DYNAMIC STUDIES IN TIMOTHY & TITUS

BRINGING GOD'S WORD TO LIFE

FRED A. SCHEEREN

WESTBOW
PRESS®
A DIVISION OF THOMAS NELSON
& ZONDERVAN

WestBow Press books may be ordered through booksellers or by contacting:

WestBow Press
A Division of Thomas Nelson & Zondervan
1663 Liberty Drive
Bloomington, IN 47403
www.westbowpress.com
844-714-3454

ISBN: 978-1-6642-1108-7 (sc)
ISBN: 978-1-6642-1107-0 (e)

Library of Congress Control Number: 2020921561

Print information available on the last page.

WestBow Press rev. date: 12/15/2020

DEDICATION

I DEDICATE THIS book to my lovely wife, Sally, who is a Jewish believer and Ivy League educated attorney. She has stood by me over the years and raised our sons in our God-loving home. The comfort of sharing our friendship and our love for Christ has encouraged me greatly in creating this series of dynamic studies of various books of the Bible. Sally's participation in our small group studies has added a much deeper dimension of richness to the discussions. Thank you for sharing your heritage, training, and knowledge.

CONTENTS

ACKNOWLEDGMENTS

MY FRIEND, BOB Mason, who at the time I began the Dynamic Bible Studies series was in his second career as the pastor of small groups at the Bible Chapel in the South Hills of Pittsburgh, suggested the overall structure of each study. Realizing our group was doing more in-depth work than most, he asked that I include several important segments in each lesson—most specifically, the warm-up and life application phases.

Bob suggested a great resource called the *New Testament Lesson Planner* from InterVarsity Press. I have augmented this with commentaries by Dr. Charles Missler from Koinonia House, the *Wiersbe Bible Commentary*, *The MacArthur Bible Handbook* by Dr. John MacArthur, the *Bible Commentaries* of J. Vernon McGee, and the whole of Scripture itself. To make the utilization of the whole of Scripture more efficient, I have also leaned heavily on the Libronix Digital Library, perhaps the most advanced Bible software available, and other resources to help us understand how the New Testament and the Tanakh (Old Testament) fit together as one cohesive document.

I have also enjoyed the input and encouragement of my friend, Ron Jones, as I have continued to prepare these studies. Ron is a former high school principal and administrator. He is also a committed believer and daily student of God's Word. His background in education coupled with his love of God and His Word has made him a powerful force for good.

I would like to express thanks to my good friend, Gordon Haresign, for his continued support and encouragement in my efforts to produce the Dynamic Bible Studies series. Gordon's journey began with his birth in the Belgian Congo. In the following years he was a senior executive with an international accounting firm, served in the military, labored as a Bible college professor, was instrumental in the leadership of a worldwide Bible correspondence school, and currently serves as the Chairman of the Board of Directors of Scripture Union, an international Bible-based ministry. Gordon's work as a teacher, speaker, and missionary has taken him to over 50 countries on five continents. His three most recent books, *Authentic Christianity*, *Pray for the Fire to Fall* and his current work on Paul's letters to the Thessalonians which will soon be in print, should be required reading for all believers. Speaking of the Dynamic Bible Studies series he has written, "These are among the finest, if not the finest, inductive Bible studies available today. I strongly endorse them."

I would also like to express my appreciation to my two proof-readers. This includes:

- Cynthia Nicastro, an intelligent, ardent and devoted student of the Scriptures and a meticulous grammarian.

- My wife Sally, a Jewish believer and Ivy League educated lawyer who was law review in law school, worked for the Superior Court of the State of Pennsylvania, and is now in private practice.

May God bless you, inspire you, teach you, and change your life for the better as you work through these lessons.

PREFACE

Welcome to what I hope you find to be a most enjoyable and enlightening study of three letters written by one of the most intelligent, highly educated, well-read and influential men in history. This man's life was changed from that of a zealous, violent, murderous enemy of the early Jewish and Gentile believers to one of the most dedicated followers of the Jewish Messiah. These letters are part of the group of documents that today is known as "The Bible" and are referred to as the Books of First Timothy, Second Timothy and Titus.

As we consider how these books of the Bible fit into the whole of the New Testament and the Tanakh (the name used by Jews for the Old Testament, used here to emphasize the Jewishness of the Scriptures), we need to realize a number of things. We should stand in awe of this collection of 66 books, written over thousands of years by at least 40 different authors. Every detail of the text is there by design. It explains history before it happens, and comes to us from outside the dimension of time. It is, in short, the most amazing, most authenticated, and most accurate book available in the world.

If this claim is not strong enough, add to it the indisputable fact that the words contained therein have changed more lives than any others now in existence.

While the Judeo-Christian Scriptures are demonstrably perfect, my prepared studies are not. There is no way I or anyone else could possibly incorporate the depth of the text into individual sessions. I simply desire to provide a vehicle for others to use in their investigation of the Scriptures as they incorporate these timeless truths into their lives.

Speaking of small groups, Dr. Chuck Missler, a former Fortune 500 CEO, said, "I experienced more growth in my personal life as a believer by participating in small group Bible studies than anything else." I believe you may find this to be true in your experience and encourage you to be an active participant in such a mutually supportive, biblically-based group.

GROUND RULES

I DESIGNED THE first portion of each study to encourage readers to think about their personal situation. I designed the second portion to help people understand what the text says and how it relates to the whole of Scripture. And finally, each lesson ends with a discussion designed to help people apply that lesson.

You will notice that, in most instances, I have included the citation, but not the actual text of the Scripture we are considering. I did this on purpose. I believe we all learn more effectively if we have to dig out the text itself. As a byproduct of that exercise, we become more familiar with this marvelous book.

Scripture references are preceded or followed by a question or series of questions. Again, this is on purpose. I have also found that people seem to learn most effectively when employing the Socratic Method. That is, instead of telling someone what the text says and how it relates to other texts and life, they will remember it better if they answer questions about it and ferret out the information for themselves.

In a few instances, I have inserted additional commentary or partial answers to some of the questions to help the group get the most out of the study.

It is my intention and suggestion that the various scripture references be read out loud as part of each session. Shorter passages might be read by one participant, while anything over two or three verses might serve everyone better if one member reads one verse and another reads the next until the passage is completed. This keeps everyone involved. After reading these passages, I intend that how they relate to the primary Scripture at hand be seriously considered. At times, this relationship seems to be available and obvious on the surface. In many other instances, the interconnectedness of the whole of Scripture and its principles are most effectively understood through deeper thought, discussion, and prayer.

In commenting on and discussing the various passages, questions, concepts, and principles in this material, it is not required that any particular person give his or her input. The reader of any passage may, but is not pressured to, give his or her thoughts to the group. This is a group participation exercise for the mutual benefit of all involved and many people in the group giving their insight into a certain verse or question will often enhance the learning experience.

I also have two practical suggestions if you work through this book in a small group setting. Every time you meet, I suggest you review the calendar and agree upon the next scheduled meeting as well as who will bring refreshments. This will help the group to run a lot more smoothly while enhancing everyone's enjoyment, experience, and expectations.

INTRODUCTION
TO PAUL'S LETTERS
TO TIMOTHY

The letters that the apostle Paul wrote to Timothy have come to be called Pastoral Epistles. While we understand what is meant by this, the moniker seems almost too tame. To the uninitiated it sometimes communicates that these are nice letters to some seminary graduate who has decided to go into the field of religion. Nothing could be further from the truth.

These letters are written by Paul. He was perhaps the most intelligent, well-educated, and accomplished man of his day. (See Philippians 3:3-8.) He became a believer after applying his great intelligence to the physical extermination of those who had decided to follow the Jewish Messiah who we know as Jesus Christ. (1 Timothy 1:12-13)

They were written to Timothy, a Jew steeped in the Old Testament Scriptures, which the Jews call the Tanakh. His mother was Jewish and his father was Greek. (Acts 16:1) As a result of the influence of his godly believing mother and grandmother as well as Timothy's familiarity with the Old Testament prophecies about the Jewish Messiah, he became a believer. He became a protégé, friend, fellow warrior and frequent companion of Paul.

The letters themselves were written in turbulent and violent times. Believers were being hunted down, imprisoned, tortured, and murdered with official approval and often sanction. Becoming a follower of Jesus was not an easy, popular or peaceful choice for one to make. It was, however, the only logical and correct one given an understanding of truth and eternity.

As we examine these letters several things become apparent. On the surface we first see their direct instruction and encouragement to Timothy. Second, we find that what God communicated to Timothy through these letters also applies to us.

Research into the Scriptures tells us that Timothy shared many characteristics that people today also have. These commonalities of the human condition make what we learn in this wonderful book even more helpful today to those individuals who have made a decision to trust Jesus Christ.

As we study this book there is nothing really new or inconsistent with the Old Testament Scriptures. Indeed, Paul's famous reference to the whole of God's Word (2 Timothy 3:16-17) referred to the Old Testament at the time the letters to Timothy were penned. Now we understand the inherent double entendre' in that statement applies to both the New and Old Testament documents. God has used the books we call First Timothy and Second Timothy to communicate His objective truth to us in a fresh way that, taken in concert with the rest of the Bible, serves to empower believers to live full and meaningful lives.

THE OCCASION OF PAUL'S FIRST LETTER TO TIMOTHY

Paul, having been released from prison, wrote his first letter to Timothy from Macedonia when Timothy was in Ephesus. It appears to have been sent to encourage his friend and protégé as well as to give him some advice from the depths of Scripture itself. The early group of believers was facing some difficult issues caused by some people engaging in what is sometimes called heterodoxy. These trouble makers were straying from the truth of God's Word and attempting to insert the stumbling blocks of misdirection associated with:

1. Legalism.

2. Speculative theology based upon giving credence to myths, legends, meaningless cognition, genealogies, and the like.

In more simple terms, believers throughout history, including today, are faced with these same issues dealing with their daily lives and conduct as well as a correct reading and understanding of God's Word. (See How to Avoid Error in the appendices of this book.)

WEEK 1

MARCHING ORDERS
1 TIMOTHY 1:1-11

Open in Prayer

Group Warm-Up Questions

Which would you rather receive from a good friend: a letter, or a phone call? Why?

What are some laws that you benefit from directly?

Read: 1 Timothy 1:1-11

Reread: 1 Timothy 1:1

Who wrote this letter?

How does the author describe himself?

By whom does he say he was appointed?

How was he appointed?

How does he describe those who appointed him?

Reread: 1 Timothy 1:2

To whom was it written?

How does Paul describe Timothy?

What three things does Paul entreat God the Father and Jesus the Son to give to Timothy through the Holy Spirit? Please make a short list.

1.

2.

3.

Why do you think the involvement of the Holy Spirit is assumed in this particular place instead of being specifically mentioned?

Does this practice sometimes occur today? How so?

Reread: 1 Timothy 1:3

Why did Paul urge Timothy to remain in Ephesus when Paul left for Macedonia?

Who, in particular, did Paul want Timothy to stop?

What were these divisive people doing that was so harmful?

How much confidence must Paul have had in Timothy to essentially use him as a "spiritual bouncer?"

Note: The original language indicates that the instructions Paul gives Timothy in his two letters to him are far more than strong suggestions. They indicate that he has been given a "charge." This is a military term and he has been given strict orders from a superior officer.

How does this knowledge add to your understanding of what we are reading today as well as the rest of what we see in the letters to Timothy?

Are believers today receiving this same charge through the Word of God as expressed in these two books of the Bible?

Reread: 1 Timothy 1:4

As we read this verse we should remember:

1. Ephesus, the great city in which Timothy worked, was the center of the mystery religions of that day.

2. The myths and fables mentioned may well have been a reference to Philo. While he was brilliant he was also wrong and misled. Surprisingly Jewish, he "spiritualized" the Tanakh and taught that clear statements of fact and history were only allegory. This then gave license to his students to disregard the historically accurate book of Genesis and anything else with which they were uncomfortable.

3. The genealogies or spiritual pedigrees causing confusion might refer to those taking great pride in their religious degrees, confusion about Israel and the Church, or "New Age" teachings.

What three specific things were the people whose teaching were "contrary to the truth" doing? Please make a list and in your own words describe why each of these practices is, at the minimum, a waste of time.

1.

2.

3.

Why is such misdirection so destructive?

According to this verse, what do such time wasting discussions not do?

Can you think of times in the world today when such discussions are an obstacle to people living a life of faith in God? Please discuss some examples.

What false doctrines or teachings still plague some churches today?

Chuck Missler said, "Too often our churches are places for entertainment rather than enlightenment and enrichment from the Word of God." What are your thoughts about his statement?

Reread: 1 Timothy 1:5

What was Paul's purpose in telling Timothy to stop those people who were engaging in time-wasting and destructive discussions?

What three ingredients do we see that are part of what God wants to see us foster?

1.

2.

3.

Note: These are in direct opposition to the destruction brought about by those engaging in misdirection. We might then ask, "What three key characteristics do we NOT see in false teachers and trouble makers?" We must realize that the answer is the same as the three ingredients just listed.

Reread: 1 Timothy 1:6

How does this verse help to expand our understanding of the previous one?

This verse seems to indicate that before people decide to spend their time in meaningless discussions that they must first turn away from having a pure heart, clear conscience and genuine faith. Why do you think this might be?

What sorts of doctrines promote negative controversy in churches or groups of believers today?

Reread: 1 Timothy 1:7

How do these puffed up teachers want to be known?

Why might they want to be known in this fashion?

Why do you think they speak so confidently?

What do they actually know about God's Word and His Law?

What goals do you believe motivate the leaders you respect in the groups of believers with which you associate?

What goals do you believe motivate the leaders you respect in the believing community at large?

Reread: 1 Timothy 1:8

What do we know about God's Law and Word when used properly?

This then begs the question of how believers are to use the law. For the answer, we look to God's Holy Word itself where we find:

1. God's immutable, objective, perfect law and standards are good. See:

    • Romans 7:12.

2. It is actually impossible for a human being to act perfectly in accordance with God's Law no matter how well intended or how much effort one puts forth. See:

    • Romans 7:18.

    • Romans 8:8.

3. The law was not given to save us. It reveals the holiness of God and our inability to attain His level of holiness by our own good works as human beings. See:

    • Ephesians 2:8-9.

4. God has rescued us from this condition by His grace. Our good works cannot save us. Because of His grace we can live a life that produces good works. See:

- Acts 13:38-39.

- Colossians 3:23-24.

At this point we might also find it helpful to remember the difference between God's mercy and His grace.

God's mercy means that we do not get what we deserve.

His grace means that we get what we do not deserve.

In what way should we use God's Law today?

What impact does or should God's Law have upon your life?

For help with this let us again look to the whole of Scripture. Here we find some helpful information about the function of the Law.

The Role of the Law

1. It enumerates types of people or behaviors that are condemned by the Law. See:

- Romans 1:18-32.

- Galatians 5:19-21.

- Romans 3:23.

2. It cannot save those who are lost in sin. See:

- Galatians 2:21.

3. It exposes, restrains and convicts the lawless while revealing the need for a savior. See:

- Galatians 3:21-29.

4. One is freed from the curse of the Law when they trust Jesus Christ. See:

- Galatians 3:10-14

Note: See "How to Avoid Error" in the appendices of this book for help in this matter.

Reread: 1 Timothy 1:9

For whom is God's law specifically not intended?

Reread: 1 Timothy 1:9-11

For whom is God's law specifically intended? Please make a list.

1.

2.

3.

4.

5.

6.

7.

8.

9.

10.

11.

12.

13.

14.

15.

Reread: 1 Timothy 1:10-11

We have been provided with a list of at least 15 behaviors, attitudes and choices engaged in by those for whom the law has been provided. What is the one overriding characteristic of the things that these people do?

Conversely, what one overriding characteristic should be evident in the lives and choices of sincere believers?

Application Questions

With what unique task has God entrusted you?

Who is someone you can write a letter of encouragement to this week?

What steps can you take to make sure your motives are from a pure heart, a good conscience, and a sincere faith?

Close in Prayer

GOD'S GRACE AND DISCIPLINE IN BATTLE
1 TIMOTHY 1:12-20

Open in Prayer

Group Warm-Up Questions

Who are some people you know whose lives were dramatically changed at some point? How did this happen?

What sorts of people try your patience the most?

Read: 1 Timothy 1:12-20

Reread: 1 Timothy 1:12

Why did Paul thank Jesus?

What three things did Jesus specifically do for Paul as mentioned in this verse?

1.

2.

3.

To what did God appoint Paul?

To what service has God appointed you?

Reread: 1 Timothy 1:13

What terrible things did Paul once do?

Why did God have mercy upon Paul?

Did Paul actually have good intentions when he was throwing believers in prison, confiscating their homes and possessions, and arranging their murders? Please explain.

How and when has God shown you mercy?

Reread: 1 Timothy 1:14

How did Paul describe the Lord's attitude toward him?

With what did the Lord fill Paul?

Where did the things the Lord filled Paul with come from?

Hint: See Galatians 5:22-23 as you construct your answer.

Suggestion: It is a good practice to memorize these verses. One can pray about them to be sure the Holy Spirit is active in their lives and producing good fruit. A person can also use these verses as a litmus test to see if they are allowing God to transform their lives into one of victory.

Note: An examination of the original language helps to drive home the point being made in this verse. Paul uses the Greek prefix *huper* in his reference to faith in this verse. *Huper* is essentially translated to mean "super" in English. This is not apparent in many translations where the translators have attempted to make the sentence flow more readily into everyday language. However, God has used the Greek here and in some other places to make a very strong point. We see this in the following references. For the purpose of emphasis after citing each verse I have included the quite literal meaning. Please look up each verse in your Bible as you go through this to add clarity to the application and meaning.

1. In 1 Timothy 1:14 this would appear as "super-increase in faith and love."

2. In 2 Thessalonians 1:3 this would appear as "super-increase in faith."

3. In Ephesians 1:19 this would read "super-abounding power."

4. In Romans 8:37 we would see this as "super-conqueror."

What impact does understanding this information from the original text and depth of meaning have upon you?

Reread: 1 Timothy 1:15

With what one short statement does Paul sum up the purpose of the life, death, and resurrection of Jesus?

How does Paul consider himself in comparison to all other human beings?

Based on what you know about Paul, why did he feel this way?

Reread: 1 Timothy 1:16

How was God's purpose in showing His mercy to Paul?

Why was this so effective at the time?

Can you think of contemporary situations when this has been true? Please give an example.

In what way has God used you as an example so that others might believe?

Reread: 1 Timothy 1:17

Why do you think Paul breaks into praise at this point in his letter to Timothy?

What attributes of God does Paul include in his praise of Him? Please make a list.

1.

2.

3.

4.

5.

6.

7.

How do these attributes of God encourage you?

In what way is God the King of your life?

Is Jesus the Lord of your life? If so, what does this mean to you?

Reread: 1 Timothy 1:18

On what did Paul base the instructions he gave to Timothy?

Why was God giving Timothy these instructions (through Paul)?

Obviously, God knew that He was going to use Timothy to fight His battles. How does this apply to believers today?

What do you fight in your life as a believer?

Make no mistake about it. We are in a Cosmic battle whether we realize it or not. As we have already noted, Timothy, at the point this letter was written to him was fighting the battle in Ephesus. In Paul's letter to the Ephesians God gives them direct orders as they move into and continue in battle. An examination of Ephesians 6:10 in the original language shows:

1. These are commands from God, not just suggestions.

2. Believers are to be continually strong.

3. They are to take positive action by following these commands.

Please read Ephesians 6:10-18 to see these orders.

Note: Some believers, eager for the battle, particularly like Revelation 17:14 where it says "They will fight against the Lamb. But the Lamb, together with His called, chosen and faithful followers, will defeat them, for He is Lord of lords and King of kings." GNT

Reread: 1 Timothy 1:19

What two primary directives did Paul give Timothy?

1.

2.

Does this also apply to us today? How so?

This verse says that some people have deliberately (NLT) violated their consciences. How might they have done this?

What is the significance of the Scripture telling us that this violation of their consciences was "deliberate?"

Why is it so important that we realize this violation was an overt action of the will of these people?

What was the result when these people violated their consciences?

What do you take this to mean?

What happens when people do this today? Please think of an example and discuss:

1. What it means for the people who do this.

2. What it means for the community of believers with whom they are associated.

3. How it impacts the non-believers who are always observing the lives of believers.

Read: Philippians 4:8

This verse taken in concert with 1 Timothy 1:19 infers that clinging to one's faith in Jesus and keeping one's conscience clear is also a matter of the will. What are your thoughts about this?

What distractions do people sometimes allow to draw them away from their faith?

Larry Norman, the "Father of Christian Rock," said that our enemy sometimes employs misdirection as an effective tool against followers of the Way. How and when have you seen this happen?

How does the principle in Philippians 4:8 help us guard against this?

How and why do some people shipwreck their faith?

Reread: 1 Timothy 1:20

What two examples does Paul give of people who violated their consciences?

We should also note here that Paul did not hide the identity of these or other destructive people for "their protection." Instead, he exposed them for the good of the body of believers.

See:

1 Corinthians 5:1-5

2 Timothy 4:14

Acts 5:1-11

What should we learn from this in the life of what is called the "church" today?

What two actions did Paul take when these people made such a negative choice?

Note: In this type of instance it appears that the people in question have made an overt decision to go beyond the remedies available to them as referenced in:

James 5:16

Romans 12:2

Read:

Proverbs 13:20

Proverbs 14:7

Proverbs 25:26

Psalm 1:1-4

Psalm 119:115

Psalm 26:4-5

1 Corinthians 5:11-13

1 Corinthians 5:13

2 Corinthians 6:14

2 Peter 3:17

Numbers 16:1-35

How should we respond today when people in a group of believers also make such negative choices?

If we respond in accordance with Scripture as Paul did, what impact does it have upon the faithful believers in the group?

How does it impact a group of believers if we respond in direct contradiction to the Scriptures in a disobedient and weak-minded fashion? (That is, what happens when we allow these people to remain as active participants, treating them as legitimate and faithful followers?)

How does it impact the effectiveness of the group if these people who have violated and continue to violate their consciences are seen by nonbelievers as representatives of what it means to be followers of Jesus?

Please discuss examples of when you have seen this handled in both ways and the impact it had.

Read:

Colossians 3:23-24

Colossians 4:5-6

Ephesians 4:29-32

What further light do these verses shed upon this subject?

Application Questions

What steps can you take today to ensure that your faith is on the proper course and not in danger of being shipwrecked?

For what grace and/or mercy that God has shown you do you want to thank Him today?

What events or experiences in your life can you use to encourage others to believe?

Close in Prayer

DRESS AND COMPORTMENT FOR SUCCESS
1 TIMOTHY 2:1-15

Open in Prayer

Group Warm-Up Questions

What are some of the controversial issues in today's culture?

What do you like or dislike about the worship in the church you attend?

How would you characterize the worship in the church you attend?

What examples can you think of that show the impact of one's dress or appearance in the society or sub-groups of society in which you live and move?

Read: 1 Timothy 2:1-15

Reread: 1 Timothy 2:1

What does Paul first urge Timothy to do?

Upon whose behalf does he urge him to do this?

What three things does Paul say should be part of these prayers? Please enumerate.

1.

2.

3.

Looking at these elements one by one, why do you think each of them is important in such prayers? Please explain.

What do we learn from the priority Paul gives to prayer?

Reread: 1 Timothy 2:2

Who next does Paul urge Timothy to pray for?

Why do you think this group is second in line?

What four requests does Paul say should be part of believer's prayers for this group of people?

1.

2.

3.

4.

Note: In his commentary on the letters to Timothy, Dr. Charles Missler made a statement that incorporated something that J. Vernon McGhee wrote. Chuck said: "I believe we are going to see more persecution of Christians in this country in the future. I join J. Vernon McGee in his view that this will probably not include many church members: "the liberal Church is so compromised today that they will go along with whatever comes along."" (McGee, J. Vernon, Thru The Bible, Thomas Nelson Publishers, Nashville, TN, 1983, Vol V, p. 436.)

What are your thoughts about these dual statements?

Reread: 1 Timothy 2:3-4

How does God feel about the prayers mentioned in the first two verses of today's study?

What two specific things does God desire for all people?

1.

2.

Why is it sometimes hard for believers as human beings to understand and accept this?

Read:

John 3:16

John 12:32

1 John 2:2

1 John 4:14

Revelation 3:20

If God wants all people to be saved, why aren't they?

Reread: 1 Timothy 2:5

How many ways are there in which a person might be reconciled to God?

How is this way described in this portion of God's Word?

How might you put this into your own words?

Why is this truth so difficult for many people to accept?

Have you ever served as a mediator between two people? If so, how did it go and what was the result?

Reread: 1 Timothy 2:6

For whom did Jesus give His life?

What was the purpose of Jesus giving His life?

Does this privilege extend to you?

Now think of the most despicable human being of whom you are aware. Who is it?

How does the sacrifice of Jesus relate to them regardless of their response to it?

Why do you think this is sometimes hard for human beings to understand or accept?

Reread: 1 Timothy 2:7

Note 1: Going back to the original language we find that the word translated "preacher" (NLT) in English is *kerux* in the Greek. This was literally a herald or messenger vested with public authority who communicated the official messages of kings, magistrates, princes, or military commanders. In this role such a person conveyed a summons or command. This was a serious position with serious consequences.

Note 2: Again going back to the original Greek we find that the word translated "apostle" (NLT) in English is *apostolos* in the original language. This meant that the person was a messenger or delegate sent forth with orders from a commanding authority. In the first century AD it was specifically applied to the twelve apostles of Jesus and in larger sense to other outstanding leaders among the early believers including Barnabas, Timothy, and Silvanus.

To what group was Paul chosen to take God's message?

With what authority of position was Paul imbued?

What two specific things was Paul charged with communicating to this group?

1.

2.

Why do some people take offense at this truth?

Why do you think Paul insists upon telling his readers that he is not exaggerating?

For what reason might some of his listeners or readers have initially thought he was exaggerating?

To what scripturally consistent task would you say God has appointed you?

Reread: 1 Timothy 2:8

What three things did Paul want people to incorporate as part of their worship?

1.

2.

3.

Taking each of these ingredients individually, please explain what you see as the impact and importance of each one.

Note: From this verse, again taken within the context of the whole of Scripture, we should see that the state of one's heart and attitude is the most important part of worship and prayer. Indeed, when observing various postures during prayer we see many positions in the Judeo-Christian Scriptures including:

1. Lifting of one's hands in 1 Timothy 2:8.

2. Standing with outstretched hands in 1 Kings 8:22.

3. Kneeling in Daniel 6:10.

4. Standing in Luke 18:11.

5. Sitting in 2 Samuel 7:18.

6. Bowing of the head in Genesis 24:26.

7. Lifting the eyes in John 17:1.

8. Falling on the ground in Genesis 17:3.

Note: Before proceeding through the rest of this chapter we must first understand the cultural situation in which Paul and those to whom he was writing were living.

1. Women at that time were generally not given the opportunity to be part of the educational system. They were generally not represented as teachers or students in the halls of higher learning. For instance there were no women at all referenced as part of the Jewish Sanhedrin. However, we do see women playing important and vital cultural and spiritual roles throughout the New and Old Testaments. (See Acts 16:14, Philemon 1:1-2, 2 Kings 5:3-4, Exodus 15:20-21.) We should also realize:

- In the Old Testament many women played important roles as in the personages of Ruth, Deborah and Queen Esther.

- Jesus first overtly revealed His role as Messiah to a woman in John 4:25-26.

- It was a woman who first recognized Jesus' prophecy of His upcoming death in John 12:7.

- Several women were at the cross.

- Women were the first to carry the news of His resurrection.

2. A woman of God was described in Proverbs 31. Time has not negated the Word of God. Culture has developed to the point where we see women in further expanded and scripturally sound roles.

3. Women adorning themselves in ways Paul warned against were, at the time this was written, often involved in prostitution. We see this in:

- The pagan culture then existent in Ephesus where Timothy was working. It was common for a young woman to begin her working life as a temple prostitute and eventually marry with no negative feelings directed toward her because of her previous behavior.

- Proverbs 7:6-27.

- Isaiah 3:16 where Israel is being compared to a prostitute.

Reread: 1 Timothy 2:9

How did Paul say that women should dress?

Note: Going back to the original language can also give us some help with this verse.

The word translated "adorn" in English, as used in the KJV 1900, comes from the Greek word kosmeo which literally means "to arrange or put in order."

The word translated as "modest" in English, also as used in the KJV 1900, was *kosmios* in the Greek and means "well arranged."

The Greek word *kosmios* comes from the Greek word *kosmos* and literally means to bring order out of chaos. It is the root of the English word "cosmetics."

The word translated into English as "sober" or with "sobriety," again as used in the KJV 1900, comes from the Greek word *sophrosune* which means "having a sound mind, good sense and self-control."

The reference to "braided hair" in the KJV simply has to do with hair styles.

In the cultural situation in Ephesus at the time 1 Timothy 2:9 was written, women adorned themselves provocatively as either prostitutes or for show. What do you think this means for people today?

What impact does it have upon people when a person, man or woman, dresses in a slovenly fashion today?

How does it impact people today when someone to whom they are relating is groomed well and dresses tastefully?

Reread:

Colossians 4:5-6

1 Peter 3:1-6

What insight does this give us into our attire and adornment today? (Remember that we must see Scripture as a whole.)

Note: We have a dear friend who was one of the five General Superintendents of the Worldwide Nazarene denomination. These five people essentially control the denomination on an international basis. The whole denomination for many years took 2 Timothy 2:9 out of the context of the whole of Scripture. As a result, for many years, they frowned upon any form of adornment or fine clothing up to and including wedding rings. Our friend was one of the first people in that denomination to take, what was daring to them, the step of actually wearing a wedding ring. As ridiculous as it sounds, this man was attempting to take Scripture as a whole utilizing the principles we find in *How to Avoid Error* in the appendices of this book in order to be obedient to God's Word. As a result, members of the denomination began to make appropriate choices in adornment and dress and to have more of a positive impact upon culture around them.

Conversely, a negative example emanating from a misunderstanding of the whole of scripture and taking this verse out of context is sometimes also seen. There was a woman at a church we attended who made this unfortunate error and wore no makeup, did not take care of her body, wore no jewelry, did not do anything at all with her hair besides cutting and washing it, and dressed in the plainest possible clothes. By taking this verse out of context and attempting to be obedient she was actually disobedient to the totality of God's Word and found herself in the unfortunate position of repulsing non-believers and sometimes believers too.

Scripture actually tells us that there is nothing wrong with wearing jewelry and having nice clothing coupled with a proper attitude and action. In fact, it has a positive impact when properly utilized. See:

Exodus 28

Song of Solomon 1:10-11

Song of Solomon 4:9

Genesis 24:53

Isaiah 61:10

Matthew 6:28-29 (Solomon dressed well.)

John 19:23-24 (Jesus' own robe was of high quality.)

Colossians 4:5-6 (again)

1 Corinthians 10:31

Colossians 3:17

Colossians 3:23-24

Reread: 1 Timothy 2:10

In what way did Paul say women should make themselves attractive?

Does this apply to both men and women today in various cultures around the world?

Is this consistent with the whole of Scripture as you understand it?

Reread: 1 Timothy 2:11-12

How did Paul say that women of the day should learn and listen?

Note: Here again it is helpful to go back to the original language to assist us in our understanding.

The word sometimes translated "silence" (KJV 1900) in English is *hesuchia* in the Greek and literally means "peaceable" or "quietness" in the sense of not being meddlesome or intrusive.

The word sometimes translated to "subjection" (KJV 1900) or "submission" (NKJV) in English has to do with order and authority, not value or ability. Submission is not subjection. Anyone who has served in a combat unit understands this concept. This also relates to 1 Corinthians 14:40 which says "But be sure that everything is done properly and in order." NLT

The word translated into English as "teach" (NLT) comes from the Greek word *didasko*. This is also the root of the English word "didactic" which relates to a specific manner of teaching through lectures.

- Paul uses the present infinitive rather than the aorist infinitive. This indicates that women are not prohibited from teaching under appropriate conditions or circumstances.

- Women are in fact permitted to teach and teach men in the right way in the correct conditions as we see in Acts 18:24-28.

- Older women are to teach the younger women as we see in Titus 2:3-4.

- Timothy himself was taught by his mother and grandmother as we see in 2 Timothy 1:5 and 2 Timothy 3:15.

- However, this also indicates that they are not to fulfill the role of pastor or teacher in the life of the church.

How do you think 1 Timothy 2:11-12 applies to the world today knowing the meaning of the Greek and that women now have more opportunities for education and learning in many cultures around the world? Remember, God's Word does not change.

Reread: 1 Timothy 2:13-14

Is this verse an indictment of women, or is it more correctly understood in relationship to the whole of Scripture as recognition that there are actual differences between men and women extending from the physical to the emotional and mental structure and functioning of the male and female genders?

Why is it that in a marriage relationship the qualities that a man brings to the table in concert with the qualities a woman brings to the table seem to form an effective operating couple as the basis for an effective family unit?

Read:

Romans 12:6-21

1 Corinthians 12

How does this same principle act in the body of believers known as the church?

Knowing that God in His Word repeats these concepts about believers in many places, more in fact than we have cited today, what do you think about their importance?

Why do we as human beings need to be reminded of this?

Reread: 1 Timothy 2:15

What do you think Paul meant by this statement?

Note: He obviously did not mean that a woman is put in proper relationship with God simply by bearing children. It is an error to hold such a view based upon taking this one verse out of context. Women as well as men are both put right with God by trusting in Jesus Christ on a personal basis.

How does the second half of this verse apply to both men and women?

What qualities of a person should be evident in their lives if they are a follower of Jesus Christ as noted in this verse?

1.

2.

3.

4.

What does one's conduct tell the world about them?

Bringing this forward to today's world we find:

1. The culture in much of the world has changed.

2. Women as well as men are highly educated and steeped in the Word of God and are being used extensively in His service. Some of the women of God included in this group include:

   • Kay Arthur.

   • Anne Graham Lotz.

- Joyce Meyer.

- Jan Markell.

- My own wife Sally, an ivy-league educated attorney who has studied God's Word several hours a day for over four decades.

- The many women in various occupations and areas of life both in the work place and at home who are devoted to and serving God.

3. Whether one is willing to admit it or not we see a developing world culture that is somewhat schizophrenic in that on one hand it recognizes and celebrates diversity while on the other it denies that there is any real difference between a man and a woman. Scripture and actual experience tell us that there is in fact a difference.

   - Developmental anthropologists, biologists and psychologists who study this matter have found that while in the womb developing males are the recipients of a chemical bath that enables them to be extremely effective at linear thought. This same chemical bath means that they are generally not as good at handling multiple inputs and simultaneously attending to multiple concepts and events at the same time. Women, however, absent this chemical bath, are much more competent in handling several things at once.

4. The existent differences between men and women enable them each to be effective in certain ways separately and to have a positive impact when yoked together in life, marriage and ministry. They complement and help each other. In God's Word we find that:

- Both men and women are created in God's image. (Genesis 1:26-27)

- The use of the word "submission" (1 Timothy 2:11 NKJV) is also seen in relationship to God the Father and Jesus the Son. It relates to proper roles and responsibilities and is actually a military term as already mentioned. (We can see this principle conceptually in Matthew 26:39, Ephesians 5:22-33, Philippians 2:5-8, Genesis 2:18, Genesis 2:24, 1 Peter 3, Romans 12:1-2, Titus 2:3-6) This list is certainly not exhaustive. Books have and will be written examining the biblical roles of men and women. Better yet, follow the admonition of Acts 17:11 and study the Scriptures yourself with the aid of a good concordance to be sure that you understand these roles from God's perspective.

5. As already mentioned the term "submit" as seen in Colossians 3:18 (NLT) is actually a military term indicating an effective order of battle and operation. Men and women are thus seen to each have roles in which they are generally more effective than their gender counterparts alone. The positive impact of this is multiplied when men and women work together with their special gifts and abilities in a common effort to communicate God's message of life, truth and freedom.

6. So we don't miss it, we should realize that there are many women today engaged in serious and effective levels of ministry in ways that were perhaps not dreamed of by the general populace in the first century AD.

7. In all areas of interaction people can and should dress for success. There exists an excellent book by that title written by John Malloy. He undertook an in-depth study of the way one's dress and adornment impacted their success with various groups of people. This body of work has helped many people have a greater impact upon the world in which they live and work. Believers are admonished to similarly be wise as we see in God's Word. (Take a look at Colossians 4:5-6 again.)

8. Acts 17:11 is for both men and women at any point of their lives regardless of their perceived position or power. We are all to search God's Word and see it as a whole as we live life the way He intends.

9. The word translated "saved" (1 Timothy 2:15 NLT) in English appears as *sozo* in the Greek. It is of great importance to realize that this word literally means "to rescue, to preserve safe and unharmed, to heal, or deliver from." It also appears frequently in the New Testament without any reference to spiritual salvation as well as to it. In the following verses it appears without a spiritual connotation:

- Matthew 8:25.

- Matthew 9:21-22.

- Matthew 10:22.

- Matthew 24:22.

- Matthew 27:40.

- Matthew 27:42.

- Matthew 27:49.

- 2 Timothy 4:18.

10. Not all men and women are meant for marriage or parenthood. See:

- 1 Corinthians 7:25-40.

11. Women are "saved" in a spiritual sense the same way as men. Not by having babies. See:

- Acts 16:30-31.

- Ephesians 2:8-10.

- John 3:16.

- John 14:6.

- Romans 10:10

12. Both women and men who trust God are expected to evidence that relationship in their daily lives. See:

- 2 Corinthians 5:17.

- Romans 12:2.

- Matthew 5:14-16.

- 2 Peter 1:3-8.

Taking all of the above into account in concert with the whole of Scripture, what do you think Paul meant when he said "But women will be saved through childbearing, assuming they continue to live in faith, love, holiness, and modesty"? (1 Timothy 2:15 NLT)

Please explain.

Can you think of a time or times when the way you dressed and/or comported yourself had a positive impact upon the situation in which you were involved? Please give an example.

Application Questions

For what national and international leaders can you pray this week?

How can you focus your attention on your life, actions and worship of God over outward appearance?

Close in Prayer

WEEK 4

LEADERSHIP
1 TIMOTHY 3:1-16

Open in Prayer

Group Warm-Up Questions

What were some of the qualifications you had to meet for your job?

What important qualities should managers possess?

Read 1 Timothy 3:1-16

Reread: 1 Timothy 3:1

What did Paul say about a person who desires to be a leader in the body of believers?

Note: J. Vernon McGee pointed out that in the Word of God a leader in the church was never called "Reverend." That title applies only to God, as seen in "revered," a form of the same word commonly used in English. "Revered" actually means "deep respect, admiration and veneration." The form of the word in the title "Reverend" actually literally means "terrible or one that incites terror." Self-veneration of those in positions of leadership led to many problems in groups of believers in the early church (as seen in Revelation 2:6, Revelation 2:15, Revelation 2:20 with the Nicolaitans.) This problem is also seen at other various places in Scripture and continues to pop up today.

Can you think of times in your experience when you have seen such a problem arise? Please explain.

Why do you think this difficulty seems to arise again and again?

How do 2 Timothy 3:16-17 and Acts 17:11 go a long way toward preventing this type of error?

Why do you think this is so?

Further Note on the Titles Seen in Today's Passage

The terms variously translated to the English words bishop, elder, or pastor were synonymous in the New Testament. Among the early believers a bishop never had actual authority over other leaders. It is of interest to understand the literal meaning of the Greek words used for these roles in the New Testament.

The Greek word *episkope* is most often translated as "bishop" (1 Timothy 3:1 NKJV) and literally means "overseer" in English.

The Greek word *presbuteros* translates to "elder" (1 Timothy 5:17 NLT) and literally means "old man" in English.

The Greek word *poimen* translates to "pastor" (Ephesians 4:11 NLT) in English and literally means "shepherd."

We should also realize that a pastor is automatically expected to be a teacher and a continual student of God's Word. We see this dual role in Ephesians 4:11.

What further insights do you gain from this understanding of the original language?

Read:

Ephesians 4:11

1 Timothy 4:6

2 Timothy 2:15

2 Timothy 2:24

Titus 2:1

Based upon these few verses do you think the primary responsibility of an elder might be said to be teaching and preaching?

Read: Ephesians 4:11-12

What is God's ultimate purpose in using various leaders among believers?

Reread: 1 Timothy 3:2-7

What qualities must a person who desires to be a leader in the body of believers possess? Please make a list and in doing so be sure to include the converse of the qualities that should be avoided.

1.

2.

3.

4.

5.

6.

7.

8.

9.

10.

11.

12.

13.

14.

Why, in your opinion, are these particular qualities so important?

What qualities must a person who desires to be such a leader not possess? Please enumerate those specifically cited.

1.

2.

3.

4.

5.

6.

Why is it so important that leaders do not have these qualities?

Why is good family management a qualification of this type of leadership?

Why is it important that a leader not be a new believer? Have you seen situations when this was a problem? Please give an example if you have observed one.

Note: The topic of divorce as it relates to leaders in the body of believers sometimes comes up in the midst of this discussion. Read the following verses and discuss what they mean in the context of this:

Matthew 5:31-32

Matthew 19:9

1 Corinthians 7:15

Reread: 1 Timothy 3:5

Also read: 1 Peter 5:3

What do you think these verses mean when taken together?

Might this role be described as a "loving shepherd"? Why or why not?

Reread: 1 Timothy 3:6

Also read: Proverbs 16:18

What do these verses mean to you when taken together?

Reread: 1 Timothy 3:7

What does it mean to you when a person has a "good" reputation?

Does it mean they pay their bills?

Does it mean that they are regarded for honesty even by unbelievers?

Does it mean they have a "wholesome" character?

How might you define a "wholesome" character?

Why must a leader have a good reputation?

What happens if a leader in the body of believers does not have a good reputation?

What is the impact when a leader in the body of believers has a stellar reputation?

How does this impact those in the community of believers?

Reread: 1 Timothy 3:8-12

Note: The Greek word *diakonos* is translated to "deacons" (1 Timothy 3:8, 10 & 12 NLT) in English and literally means "servants." While deacons do not have the same authority as elders, they still must meet certain qualifications. The origin of this word is often said to emanate from Acts 6 where we see deacons essentially acting as assistants to the apostles. It is of great note that Paul, perhaps the most intelligent and highly educated man of his time and who also was used by God to produce much of the New Testament, was called a deacon. (In the New Testament we see "deacons" often taking an active part in leadership and most certainly as servants. We see Paul referred to as performing the functions of this role in 1 Corinthians 3:5-9. Most revealing of all, the Greek word from the original text that most every version of the Bible translates as "servants" (NLT, NCV, ESV, NASB 1995, NIV) in 1 Corinthians 3:5 is, in fact, *diakonos*.)

How important, in your opinion, is the role of a deacon in the body of believers? Why?

What qualities must a deacon possess? Please make a list.

1.

2.

3.

4.

5.

6.

7.

What qualities must a deacon most pointedly not possess?

Dr. Charles Missler famously said, "A deacon who does not know the Bible is an obstacle to growth in a local assembly. Simply being a successful or popular person in business or a generous contributor does not necessarily mean they are qualified to serve as a deacon."

What do you think about what Chuck said?

Can you think of times when someone was appointed to the role of deacon but did not have the requisite knowledge of God's Word? What happened?

Conversely, can you think of an example when someone was an ardent student of God's Word, effectively applied it to their life, and became a deacon? What happened in that instance?

Reread: 1 Timothy 3:10 (I suggest you do this in several different translations of the Bible.)

1 Timothy 3:6

Proverbs 16:18

Also read:

Matthew 25:21

Why is a preliminary period of growth, experience, learning and practice important for the success of a person appointed to become a deacon?

Can you think of a time when a person was appointed to such an important role without a period of training? What happened?

Reread: 1 Timothy 3:11

What qualities must the wife of a deacon possess?

1.

2.

3.

What must the wife of a deacon most pointedly not do?

Why do you think not engaging in this particular behavior is so important?

What negative consequences emerge when someone engages in such behavior?

How does it impact the individual doing it?

How does it impact their spouse?

How does it impact the body of believers?

What message does it send to those who are not believers if it is allowed to persist?

Note: The English word "slanders" (See: 1 Timothy 3:11 NLT, NKJV) comes from the Greek word *diabolos*. *Diabolos* is also one of the titles used of Satan in God's Word. It is the root of the English word "diabolical," which in general terms is thought of as "characteristic of the Devil, or so evil as to be suggestive of the Devil" as stated in the general Google dictionary. If we look this up in other dictionaries we will see it corroborated in the Merriam-Webster dictionary, the Cambridge English Dictionary, and others.

What is the import of this term in daily life and conversation as you understand it?

Reread: 1 Timothy 3:12

Also read: Luke 16:10

What three additional qualifications must a deacon meet to be suitable for such a position?

1.

2.

3.

Please discuss why each of these in and of itself is so important.

What benefits derive to both the local and overall body of believers if these three qualities are evident in the life of person serving as a deacon?

What problems can arise if any of these criteria are not met?

Reread: 1 Timothy 3:13

What rewards does a person who does well as a deacon reap?

1.

2.

Reread: 1 Timothy 3:14-15

Why did Paul write these instructions?

Why is it so important that believers comport themselves in concert with God's standards? As you construct your answer please read:

Colossians 4:4-6

Colossians 3:23-24

Ephesians 4:29-30

Which of the character qualities needed by both overseers and deacons do you think is the most important for a leader among believers to possess?

Where does integrity stack up?

If you applied the lists of qualifications for these positions to yourself, how would you measure up?

What do you think is the one common ingredient in the lists of qualifications for leaders in the church?

If you had to pick, what role would you choose in the group of believers of which you are a part? Why?

Read: Ephesians 4:11-12

How is the "church" (Ephesians 4:11-12 NLT), defined as the corporate body of all believers, to grow?

Is this a matter of attendance at group gatherings, assets, contributions, programs, or something else?

What nourishment is required for believers on both an individual and group basis to grow according to the plan of God? Read the following verses as you prepare your answer:

Matthew 4:4

Hebrews 5:12-14

2 Timothy 3:16-17

Psalm 19:7-11

Psalm 25:4-5

Psalm 25:9-10

Psalm 94:12

Psalm 111:7-8

Psalm 112:1

Hebrews 4:12

Psalm 119

Psalm 12:6

Reread: 1 Timothy 3:16

How does Paul describe the great mystery of the faith shared by those who have come to trust Jesus Christ on a personal basis?

What are the component parts of this mystery as put forth by Paul in this verse?

1.

2.

3.

4.

5.

6.

Application Questions

What quality from the lists in 1 Timothy 3:1-16 do you want to improve in your life? How could you start?

In what way can you serve in the group of believers of which you are a part?

Close in Prayer

WARNING, TIMOTHY, WARNING!!!
1 TIMOTHY 4:1-16

Open in Prayer

Group Warm-Up Questions

Why do you think there is so much of an emphasis on physical fitness in our society?

Despite the emphasis on physical fitness in society today, why do you think there is such an epidemic of diabetes, heart disease, obesity, and drug abuse?

What qualities do you look for in a minister or pastor?

Read: 1 Timothy 4:1-16

Reread: 1 Timothy 4:1

What does the Holy Spirit tell us will happen as we move toward what the Scriptures call the "last times" (1 Timothy 4:1 NLT), the "latter days" (Daniel 2:28 KJV), "latter times" (1 Timothy 4:1 KJV 1900), or "last days" (2 Peter 3:3-4 ESV and 1 Peter 1:20 NLT).

Note: In colloquial and general usage this period of time is simply often spoken of in English as the "end times."

What does the Bible version you are using call this period of time?

What do you understand the terminology about this period of history to mean?

What specific three things does the Holy Spirit tell us that some people will do in the "last times (1 Timothy 4:1 NLT)?"

1.

2.

3.

Reread: 1 Timothy 4:2

What three personal characteristics do we find in people who engage in the negative behaviors described in 1 Timothy 4:1?

1.

2.

3.

Do you think the qualities of these people referenced in 1 Timothy 4:2 were caused by them following the practices in 1 Timothy 4:1 or might it have been the other way around? Please explain the reasoning behind your conclusion.

Can you think of a time when this has happened or is happening in the world today? Please give an example.

What does Paul say about the consciences of hypocrites and liars who have engaged in the practices cited in 1 Timothy 4:1?

How does a person act when their conscience is dead?

Read:

Acts 20:28-31

2 Corinthians 11:13-15

Deuteronomy 13:12-18

Leviticus 17:7

Deuteronomy 32:15-17

Psalm 106:33-37

2 Peter 2:1-3

Explanatory Note: The problem with false teachers was not new to the believers in Ephesus nor is it new to us today. We should realize that:

1. These false teachers invade groups of people who are following God.

2. They infiltrate believing groups and then seem to arise from within them.

3. Like a cancer, their evil efforts must be stopped from advancing within groups of faithful believers.

4. The many biblical references to false teachers apply in many ways:

   - To the situation at hand when the passage was written.

   - To all groups of believers in existence at the time the passage was written.

   - To people following God prior to the passage being recorded.

   - To groups of believers to come in the years following the time the passage was written.

   - To the "later days" (Daniel 2:28 KJV) when Scripture tells us that problems of this nature will increase.

Fortunately, God's Word provides specific direction about how to handle this situation when it arises. While the following verses are not exhaustive, they do provide a foundation of knowledge, information and instruction about how to regard and handle such people and problems when they inevitably arise.

Matthew 7:15-16

Ephesians 5:11

Galatians 1:8

Matthew 16:12

Titus 1:10-13

Titus 1:13-14

Leviticus 18:29 (For context and application see Leviticus 18:1-30.)

Titus 1:15-16

Romans 16:17-18

1 Kings 22:46

Titus 3:10-11

2 Thessalonians 3:6

1 Corinthians 15:33

Hebrews 6:4-6

1 Corinthians 5:1-6

Numbers 15:30

1 Corinthians 5:9-13

Titus 2:7-8

2 Timothy 4:2-4

Ephesians 4:14-15

2 Timothy 2:15

Acts 17:11

1 Timothy 5:20-21

How would you summarize the biblical solution to this type of problem when it rears its ugly and divisive head? Please make a list of what you understand the Scripture to say in regard to this matter.

1.

2.

3.

4.

5.

6.

7.

Note: You might also find it helpful to again review *How to Avoid Error* in the appendices of this book.

One might also notice in 1 Timothy 5:20-21 that an open and public repudiation of those causing problems in a fellowship of believers seems to be in order according to the Word of God. Why might this be an important thing to remember and do?

Why are many modern "churches" hesitant to do this?

What problems arise when a group of believers fails to recognize, publicly rebuke, and rid themselves of false teachers?

Reread: 1 Timothy 4:3

What two specific things did Paul predict would be claimed and encouraged by the hypocrites and liars mentioned in 1 Timothy 4:2 (NLT)?

1.

2.

Do we witness these practices in the world today? When and where?

What is the impact when these practices are adhered to today? Please give some specific examples.

Do you see the results of these practices in the world today as being helpful or destructive?

What does Paul say about the foods mentioned?

Read:

Genesis 1:26-28

Genesis 2:18

Genesis 2:22-24

Matthew 19:10-12

1 Corinthians 7

Mark 10:6-9

Hebrews 13:4

Ephesians 5:22-23

1 Corinthians 10:31

Colossians 3:23-24

According to these verses, how does God seem to feel about these matters?

What seems to be the one overriding guiding principle?

Reread: 1 Timothy 4:4-5

Also read:

Mark 7:14-23

Acts 10:9-15

1 Corinthians 10:23-33

Romans 14:1-12

Colossians 2:16-17

How should we regard things created by God?

In what fashion should we receive these things?

What is it that makes something acceptable according to God's standards?

Reread: 1 Timothy 4:6

What results did Timothy expect when he explained these things to the Believers over whom he had responsibility?

1.

2.

3.

Does this hold true for leaders in groups of believers today? How so?

Chuck Missler warned people about what he called "one verse theology." What do you think he means by this?

Read:

Matthew 4:4

1 Peter 2:2-3

Jeremiah 15:16

Acts 17:11

According to these verses in what way can believers be sure to follow the truths of God's Word?

Reread: 1 Timothy 4:7

What are believers to not do?

Can you think of times when you have seen people doing this?

What is the impact of people engaging in this type of behavior? Please list the results you can think of.

1.

2.

3.

4.

5.

6.

Conversely, what are believers to do?

Reread: 1 Timothy 4:8

How is physical training like training for godliness?

How is training for godliness superior to physical training?

Reread: 1 Timothy 4:9

Why do you think the Word of God emphasizes the saying in 1 Timothy 4:8?

Why do you think that we as human beings need to have this principle emphasized to us?

Reread: 1 Timothy 4:10

For what reason did Paul and Timothy work so hard?

Reread: 1 Timothy 4:11

What did Paul tell Timothy to do in regard to the truths he wrote to him about in the verses under consideration today?

Why do you think Timothy was to "insist" (1 Timothy 4:11 NLT) that the believers with whom he was associated learn these truths?

How does this relate to leaders and groups of believers today?

What happens when leaders do not insist that those in their group learn these truths?

Why does God regard it as so important that believers make these truths a part of their lives?

Reread: 1 Timothy 4:12

Note: At the time this was written, a youth was referred to as someone less than 40 years of age.

In what specific areas of life did Paul tell Timothy to be an example to all believers? Please list them in your own words.

1.

2.

3.

4.

5.

6.

7.

Should all people who have trusted Jesus Christ do the same thing in their lives today? Please explain.

Read: Colossians 3:23-24

How do the concepts in this verse relate to 1 Timothy 4:12?

Reread: 1 Timothy 4:13

What three primary things was Timothy to focus on before Paul arrived?

1.

2.

3.

What is so important about these three things acting in concert that Timothy was to focus on them?

Are these three things also vital to groups of believers today? How so?

What happens in a group of believers when just one of these components is missing?

Reread: 1 Timothy 4:14

What was Timothy to not neglect?

What spiritual gift(s) do you have that you should not neglect?

Reread: 1 Timothy 4:15

Reread: Colossians 3:23-24

What was Timothy to do with his life?

Are all believers called to do the same thing in relation to their lives?

It seems to me that the term "lazy Christian" is an oxymoron. What do you think?

What do you observe about this in the real world today?

Reread: 1 Timothy 4:16

What three things does Paul admonish Timothy to do?

1.

2.

3.

Should all believers do this today?

For what two specific reasons should all believers and leaders among believers do these three things today?

1.

2.

Application Questions

What specific actions can you schedule into your daily routine to nurture your godliness?

Question 2 Part 1: For what other believers and non-believers can you set an example in speech, lifestyle, love, faith or purity?

Question 2 Part 2: How can you set the example spoken of in the first part of this question?

How can you keep watch over your life and teaching this week? (Helpful hint: See How to *Avoid Error* in the Appendices of this book.

Close in Prayer

MEN, WOMEN, WIDOWS, ELDERS, AND SLAVES

1 TIMOTHY 5:1-6:2

Open in Prayer

Group Warm-Up Questions

What groups of people are treated with special favor in society today?

Whose responsibility is it to care for the needy and elderly?

How much money do you think a pastor should make? Why?

How would you describe a person who is a "full-time" worker for God?

Read: 1 Timothy 5:1-6:2

Note: Remember the warning against "one verse theology." To successfully learn and apply God's Word to life we should view it as a whole. See *How to Avoid Error* in the appendices of this book as well as:

2 Timothy 3:16-17.

Reread: 1 Timothy 5:1

What do you think this verse presupposes about an older man to whom you might be speaking?

How are we to never speak to an older man?

Why do you think God is so emphatic in telling us that this is to never happen?

How does it impact an older man when you speak harshly to him?

How does it impact you if you speak harshly to an older man?

How does it impact those who observe your behavior if they see you speaking harshly to an older man?

Conversely, how are we instructed to speak to an older man?

Reread: 1 Timothy 5:1

How are we to speak to younger men?

What does this mean to you? Please make a list.

1.

2.

3.

4.

5.

Reread: 1 Timothy 5:2

How are we to treat older women?

What, specifically, does this mean to you?

1.

2.

3.

4.

5.

How are we to treat younger women? Please make another list. (Remember that this letter was written to Timothy, a man.)

1.

2.

3.

4.

5.

Conversely, how are we to NOT treat younger women?

How can we be sure to adhere to God's principles as we do this?

Note: Many people are familiar with the "Billy Graham Rule." When Billy got married he vowed to never be alone with another woman regardless of the circumstances.

What positive results does following such a rule produce?

What negative results have you seen occur when this rule is not followed?

Do you think this rule is a good idea or a bad one? Please explain.

Historical Background:

1. God has always had a special concern for widows and the helpless as we see in His Word going back thousands of years. See:

   - Deuteronomy 14:29 (Written about 3,500 years ago).

   - Psalm 94:1-6 (Written about 3,000 years ago).

   - Malachi 3:5 (Written about 2,400 years ago).

2. God has always demanded that widows, orphans, and the helpless receive justice and are provided for. See:

   - Deuteronomy 24:17.

   - Isaiah 1:17.

   - Deuteronomy 10:17-18.

3. There was an early concern regarding widows among believers in the first century AD. We can see this in:

- Acts 6:1.

- Acts 9:39.

Reread: 1 Timothy 5:3

To whom did Paul tell Timothy to recognize and care for?

What important qualifier to this admonition does Paul mention?

Reread: 1 Timothy 5:4

Also read:

- Exodus 20:12

- Ephesians 6:1-3

According to 1 Timothy 5:4, what should the children and grandchildren of a widow do? The Scripture breaks this down to three components. Please list them.

1.

2.

3.

Reread: 1 Timothy 5:5

How does Paul define a "true widow" (1 Timothy 5:5 NLT)? What are the component characteristics?

1.

2.

3.

4.

Reread: 1 Timothy 5:6

What are the characteristics of a woman who is not a "true widow?"

Reread: 1 Timothy 5:7

What did Paul instruct Timothy to do with the instructions about how to treat "true widows?"

What negative consequences can occur when "true widows" are not given the help that God requires?

What sorts of people besides those who are not "true widows" are tempted to misuse their idle time?

Reread: 1 Timothy 5:8

What do we learn about those who refuse to care for their relatives, especially those living in their own household?

1.

2.

What presuppositions are endemic to this statement?

What do you think it means to care properly for needy family members?

Which of your family members need your active care?

Read: Colossians 3:23-24

What light might these verses carry in regard to the weight each member of a household must carry?

Reread: 1 Timothy 5:9-10

Obviously, God does not regard a widow as worthy of support by the group of believers to whom she belongs simply because she lives and breathes. What conditions are mentioned in these verses that should be met for a widow to receive support? Please make a list.

1.

2.

3.

4.

5.

6.

7.

8.

9.

What are the negative consequences when a widow receives support who does not meet the qualifiers set forth in God's Word?

How does this impact believers?

How does this impact those who observe the community of believers?

Conversely, how does it impact believers and those observing them when a "true widow" who has acted in accord with God's standards for life is supported by other believers?

Reread: 1 Timothy 5:11-13

Why should younger widows not be on the list for long term support?

God's Word puts forth several reasons why this is so. Please enumerate them.

1.

2.

3.

4.

5.

6.

To what might these younger widows fall prey?

Reread: 1 Timothy 5:14

What advice does Paul tell Timothy to give to the younger widows?

1.

2.

3.

What did Paul say would be the result if the younger widows followed this admonition?

Read Proverbs 31:10-31 for more insight into Paul's advice and the impact a woman of God can have upon her husband and family.

Reread: 1 Timothy 5:15

What had already happened in Ephesus to some of the younger widows?

Given the extreme pagan and negative culture in Ephesus at the time this letter was written, what do you think these women who had already gone astray were doing?

Reread: 1 Timothy 5:16

Why did Paul encourage believing women to take care of relatives who were "true widows" (ESV, BLB)?

If you had to sum it up, how would you say God expects us to treat fellow believers?

Note: Elders were leaders in the various groups of believers who were chosen, ordained and to be used by God in the guidance and leadership of the group of which they were a part. See:

Acts 14:23.

Acts 20:17.

Acts 20:28.

Titus 1:5.

Reread: 1 Timothy 5:17

How should elders be regarded and remunerated when they do their work well?

1.

2.

Which elders should be paid with special generosity?

The New King James Version says in 1 Timothy 5:17:

"Let the elders who rule well be counted worthy of double honor, especially those who labor in the word and doctrine."

Many readers take this to mean that they should receive double the compensation of other elders. What do you think?

Reread: 1 Timothy 5:18

Also read:

Deuteronomy 25:4

1 Corinthians 9:7-14

What principle are we to apply to those working hard and doing good work while working?

Why is it important to do this?

How do you think a "Christian worker's" salary should be determined? Why?

Note 1: This is a difficult topic for many people. There is no Scriptural admonition for those following God or doing His work to live in poverty. And yet, in our society, there seems to be a general feeling that these people need not be rewarded too generously. Why do you think this feeling exists?

Note 2: Paul Anderson, the "World's Strongest Man," was a believer. He achieved this record by officially lifting 6,270 pounds off of railroad trestles and it has never been broken. (It was widely reported that he far exceeded this weight in unofficial venues.) He drove a luxurious Cadillac with a hood ornament of "Atlas." Many people criticized him for this.

After winning the Olympic gold medal for weight lifting Paul ultimately made the decision to devote his gifts to raising money to establish and fund a home for wayward boys. The Paul Anderson Youth Home still functions in Vidalia, Georgia many years after his death.

To raise these funds Paul traveled the world giving demonstrations and speaking about his sport and his faith. Besides occasionally sharing the platform with Billy Graham he was very active in the Fellowship of Christian Athletes. He made a conscious decision to forego personal wealth to support the project that God put before him.

During his travels Paul drove hundreds of thousands of miles and flew many more. He was a big man and not only needed adequate seating space when on the road, but a mode of transportation that would enable him to arrive as fresh as possible for his engagement which came in a steady stream one after the other.

What are your thoughts about his critics who thought that perhaps he should have driven a much smaller and more modest automobile?

Reread: 1 Timothy 5:19

How should accusations against an elder be handled?

Reread: 1 Timothy 5:20

Why should those who sin be reprimanded publicly?

This directive comes to us in the context of the discussion about elders as well as the community of believers as a whole.

Why is it important that it apply to elders as well as others?

What are the negative consequences when this directive from the Word of God is not followed?

How have you learned from the mistakes of others?

How have you learned from your own mistakes?

Reread: 1 Timothy 5:21

In whose presence did Paul solemnly command Timothy to follow the instructions he had just given him?

1.

2.

3.

What two important things must we not do when following God's instructions?

1.

2.

In what negative ways does favoritism impact how we treat others?

Reread: 2 Timothy 3:16-17

Read: Acts 17:11

What is to be our ultimate arbiter of truth as we relate to any and all situations in life as they apply to circumstances and people?

Reread: 1 Timothy 5:22-23

What are we to not do? In each instance please explain why.

1.

2.

3.

What does Paul tell Timothy to do? Please explain the reason for each action as you see it.

1.

2.

How do you see these instructions impacting us today?

How can we keep ourselves pure in a society that does not support God's ideals and standards?

Note: Some denominations have claimed that the wine mentioned in the biblical record was really just grape juice in an effort to stamp out alcoholism among their parishioners or to promote a policy of total abstinence from alcohol. The claim that wine produced and ingested during the time the Bible was written contained no alcohol is just not true.

As point in fact, wine is used in the Feast of Passover (in the month we call April) and the Feast of Pentecost just 7 weeks later. The Feast of Tabernacles (in the month of October) occurred at the end of the year. The only time grape juice would have been available at all was at the end of their year during the fruit harvest. Any grape juice produced would shortly begin to ferment and was turned into wine with alcohol content.

There was no grape juice left over the next year for the Feasts of Passover or Pentecost. It had been converted to wine.

This is not to say that the Scriptures encourage overindulgence. In fact, just the opposite is true. For more information and understanding on this topic see:

Leviticus 10:9

Numbers 6:2-3

Proverbs 20:1

Proverbs 23:20-21

Proverbs 31:4-5

Proverbs 31:6-7

Isaiah 5:11

Isaiah 5:22-23

Isaiah 24:9

Isaiah 28:7

Isaiah 56:10-12

Ecclesiastes 9:7

Psalm 104:14-15

Ecclesiastes 5:18

Proverbs 23:29-35

Romans 14:21

1 Corinthians 6:9-10

1 Corinthians 6:12

2 Peter 2:19

1 Corinthians 8:9-13

John 2:1-11

Matthew 26:29

Ephesians 5:18

Romans 14:22-23

1 Timothy 3:8

1 Corinthians 5:11

1 Corinthians 9:12

1 Corinthians 9:24-27

1 Corinthians 6:19-20

1 Corinthians 10:31

Colossians 3:17

How might you summarize the above references and their application for believers?

Reread: 1 Timothy 5:24-25

What is the impact of a person's sins as well as their good deeds?

Why do you think God's Word makes a direct statement about those things that are done without being obvious to those around them at the time?

In what way might our sins and/or good deeds precede us in life?

In what way might our sins and/or good deeds follow us in life?

Note: At the time Paul wrote this letter to Timothy fully 50% of the Roman Empire was comprised of slaves. While many were educated and cultured they were generally treated as property and not as human beings. Bringing this forward, hopefully most of the people reading the next two verses are now employees and not slaves.

Reread: 1 Timothy 6:1

How are slaves and generally today employees to relate to their masters and employers?

Why are they to do this?

Reread: 1 Timothy 6:2

Why do you think it is necessary for God to tell slaves and employees to not be disrespectful to their masters and employers if those in authority over them are believers?

Why do you think this tendency exists?

Why should employees or slaves work all the harder if those under whose authority they work are believers?

What is Paul's final instruction to Timothy in this verse?

Why do you think the instructions to Timothy are again reiterated in this verse? Why did God need Timothy to have them driven home again?

Why do you think God's Word continually drives home His standards and truth in a consistent fashion from the first verse in Genesis to the last in Revelation?

Application Questions

Note: Please be specific as you think about and answer the following question. Apply it to one or more specific individuals and their circumstances. Go beyond simple platitudes.

1. Considering the people in your life, in what specific way do you personally need to treat:

   • Older men?

- Younger men?

- Older women?

- Younger women?

2. In what area of life do you need to depend on God to help you keep yourself pure?

Close in Prayer

WEEK 7

LOVE OF MONEY
1 TIMOTHY 6:3-10

Open in Prayer

Group Warm-Up Questions

What evidence do you see of a love for money among your friends or coworkers?

Why do you think most people are or are not content with what they have?

Read: 1 Timothy 6:3-10

Reread: 1 Timothy 6:3

What do some people do in regard to the clear and wholesome teachings of Jesus as revealed in the Bible?

What do the clear teachings of Scripture promote?

Reread: 1 Timothy 6:4

Note: In this passage false teachers are ultimately defined as people who promote doctrines and principles that are in contradiction to the clear truths of Scripture.

What things do we learn about false teachers in the first portion of this verse?

1.

2.

3.

What are the net results when an arrogant teacher without understanding gives vent to their inclination to "quibble over the meaning of words" (1 Timothy 6:4 NLT)? Please make a list.

1.

2.

3.

4.

5.

What controversial false doctrines have you seen arise in groups of believers that you have observed or been a part?

Read:

Isaiah 8:20

2 Timothy 1:13

Acts 17:11

How does God expect us to effectively monitor what is being taught?

Chuck Missler said, "A big heart is better than a big head." What are your thoughts about his statement?

Reread: 1 Timothy 6:5

What additional characteristics are evident in false teachers?

1.

2.

3.

4.

Why do you think the misuse of godliness as a way to become wealthy is a hallmark of false teachers?

Why is it that misuse of godliness and God's truths by false teachers seem to so often result in what some have called "a fleecing of the flock?"

How could someone think that godliness was a means to financial gain?

How do some people attempt to use even true faith as a way to enrich themselves? Please explain.

At the same time, God's Word tells us that a good worker should be rewarded.

See:

Deuteronomy 25:4

1 Timothy 5:17-18

1 Corinthians 9:9-10

Note: Enemies of God's Word have, over the centuries, utilized many specious tools to lead gullible people away from life-giving faith in Jesus Christ. Some of these have included:

- The Inquisition.

- *The Last Temptation of Christ* by Nikos Kazantzakis.

- *The Passover Plot* by Hugh Schonfield.

- *Banned Books of the Bible* as presented on the History Channel.

- *The Jesus Seminar.*

- *The DaVinci Code* by Dan Brown.

- The National Geographic feature of the discredited "Gospel of Judas."

- *The Passion* by Mel Gibson in that it fails to actually define who Jesus is.

- Seminarian dissertations on meaningless and misleading subjects.

What other examples of this kind of oftentimes subtle and cloaked attack can you think of?

Reread: 1 Timothy 6:6

Also read:

John 16:33

Philippians 4:11-13

How does true godliness with contentment result in great wealth?

How does this evidence itself in the life of a believer?

Can you think of an example of this in your life? Please explain.

Is this wealth that emanates from true godliness and contentment a permanent condition for a believer or must one continually cultivate it? How so?

Why is it hard for many of us as human beings to be content?

What would make you content right now?

On a statistical basis, it is claimed that more wealthy people than poor people commit suicide. Why do you think this might be?

Reread: 1 Timothy 6:7

Also read:

Job 1:21

Ecclesiastes 5:15

Ecclesiastes 2:21

What physical possessions do each of us bring into this world?

Regardless of what we accumulate in this world, what will we take with us when we leave it?

Who do you regard as the richest person in terms of financial assets in the world?

How much will he or she take with them when they die?

How does this compare to what you will take with you when you die?

Jim Elliot, a missionary martyred as he endeavored to share God's truths with violent indigenous peoples, is famously quoted as having said "He is no fool who gives up what he cannot keep to gain what he cannot lose." Do you think he was right? How so?

What get-rich-quick schemes have you seen people fall for?

What get rich-quick-schemes have you personally fallen for, if any?

Read: Matthew 6:19-21

What can we do to build up transportable wealth that will follow us when we experience physical death?

Reread: 1 Timothy 6:8

With what two physical comforts alone should we learn to be content?

How does it impact a person when they come to this realization?

The Quakers had a saying about such things. They said, "If ever thou dost need anything, come to see me, and I will tell you how to get along without it." What do you think about this?

Writing in 1854 Henry David Thoreau said, "A man is rich in proportion to the number of things he can afford to let alone." What are your thoughts about this concept?

Reread: 1 Timothy 6:9

What happens to people who long to be rich? Please put the concepts in this verse into chronological order as presented in the biblical text. Be sure to break them down into component parts.

1.

2.

3.

4.

5.

Why do you think things progress in this fashion when a person makes their primary focus in life one of accumulating worldly wealth?

Reread: 1 Timothy 6:10

What does the Word of God say is the root of all kinds of evil?

What is the difference between loving money and being glad to use one's money for godly purposes?

What has happened to some people who have craved money above all else?

Why is it that the end result of loving money ends in ruin and many sorrows?

Can you think of examples when you have seen this happen? Please explain.

On a scale of one to ten (ten being very important), how important is money to you?

Why do you think that money is important or not very important?

What can a person do to guard against placing too much importance on their personal possessions?

Money is not inherently evil. It is simply a tool that can be used for good or ill. Chuck Missler said, "It may be alright to have what money can buy if you do not lose what money cannot buy." What do you think he meant by this?

Do you agree or disagree with what Dr. Missler said? Why?

Truths about Money

Thinking about money, we should also be aware of the following truths:

1. Wealth is not a sin. Abraham, Job and Solomon were all wealthy. See:

    - Genesis 13:2.

    - Job 1:3.

    - 1 Samuel 2:7.

    - 1 Chronicles 29:12.

    - 2 Chronicles 9:13-29.

2. Money is a gift from God. See:

    - Deuteronomy 8:11-18.

3. Believers should use their wealth as God directs and be willing to part with it if required. See:

    - Matthew 19:27.

    - Job 1:21.

4. Love of money ignores true gain. See:

    - Mark 8:36.

    - Luke 12:15-21.

5. Overconcentration on wealth obscures the simplicity of a life enjoyed. See:

   • Ecclesiastes 5:11.

   • Matthew 6:24-31.

6. Negative concentration on wealth can result in entrapment and succumbing to sinful desires with eternal consequences. See:

   • Deuteronomy 7:25.

   • Matthew 27:3-5.

   • Acts 8:20-23.

   • James 5:1-5.

7. Our real treasure is not in terms of money or possessions. See:

   • Matthew 6:26.

   • 2 Corinthians 6:10.

   • Proverbs 22:1.

   • Proverbs 3:13-14.

   • Philippians 4:19.

   • Matthew 6:33.

   • Matthew 6:19-21.

   • Ephesians 1:17-21.

While we are discussing the topic of money, we ought to turn our attention to the Biblical concept of tithing. Read:

Leviticus 27:30-32.

Deuteronomy 14:22-23.

Genesis 14:20.

Malachi 3:8-10.

2 Chronicles 31:4-6.

Matthew 23:23.

1 Corinthians 9:13-14.

1 Corinthians 16:1-2.

2 Corinthians 8:14.

Hebrews 7:5-6.

Luke 12:48.

Luke 16:1-13.

Note 1 on Tithing: From these verses a few overriding principles might arise including:

- A tenth of all is His.

- We need to be careful and systematic in our tithing.

- Keeping records can be helpful, especially if one has to give account to the tax authorities as well as to God.

- Our actual giving comes only after the return of His tenth.

Note 2 on Tithing: Some people try to make a case for tithing having been abolished with the close of the Old Testament. Such a statement, however, ignores several basic truths including:

- The Old Testament (Tanakh) and the New Testament are parts of one cohesive document.

- Nowhere in Scripture does it say that tithing no longer matters since the institution of the New Covenant.

- As point of fact, Jesus said He did not come to do away with the Old Testament, but to fulfill it. (See Matthew 5:17-20.)

Note 3 on Tithing: It is interesting in today's world that some organizations will try to tell you that theirs is the one and only place to which you should direct your tithes. Hardly a day goes by when my wife and I do not receive four or five requests for money in the mail. Some of these claim all of our tithe ought to go to them while some ask for a portion of it either after first giving to our local church or in other cases as a part of the whole. We might consider the following comments:

- The local fellowship of believers of which one is a part, commonly called a church, ought to be deserving of our support and we should provide it. If one feels that their "church" is not deserving of their support they ought to examine not only their church but themselves in making decisions about their participation with other believers as directed in God's Word (Hebrews 10:25).

- In our giving and/or tithing we should not respond merely to an apparent or stated *need*.

- We should, as Chuck Missler says, "Look for evidence that God is in the action and then join Him in what He is doing."

- The whole of Scripture is to be our guide in this as in all other endeavors.

Application Questions

What can you do to keep a proper perspective on money and possessions in your life?

About what situation in life will you ask God to help you be more content each day this week?

How can you help a fellow believer keep a proper perspective on money and possessions?

Close in Prayer

FINAL CHARGE TO TIMOTHY
1 TIMOTHY 6:11-21

Open in Prayer

Group Warm-Up Questions

What well-known people or historical figures are known to you as fighters?

What sort of goals do people in your position in life tend to pursue? (This can relate to occupation or general position in life.)

What goals do TV commercials and print ads encourage people to pursue?

Read: 1 Timothy 6:11-21

Reread: 1 Timothy 6:11

In what way does Paul refer to Timothy in this verse?

As students of the Scriptures we should understand that this is a high compliment of a sort that we find in very few other places in Scripture when applied to an outstanding personage. See:

Deuteronomy 33:1

1 Samuel 9:6

1 Kings 17:18

Nehemiah 12:24

In 1 Timothy 6:11 Paul tells Timothy to flee from certain things. This, of course, requires us to review the preceding verses to see what things Timothy is being instructed to flee from. Please read 1 Timothy 6:3-10 and list below the things he is instructed to flee from:

1.

2.

3.

4.

5.

6.

Should we also flee from these same things? Why?

Note: Fleeing in this verse is essentially a sign of wisdom, strength, as well as a means of victory.

Read the following verses and discuss the concept of victorious flight.

- 1 Samuel 19:10 (David flees when Saul tries to kill him even though David could have killed Saul.)

- Genesis 39:12 (Joseph flees another man's wife when she tries to seduce him.)

- 2 Timothy 1:7

- James 4:7

Note: To be effective in this life we must be known not just for the things in which we will not engage, but for those in which we do. These qualities can be inculcated properly only with the power we receive from the indwelling of God's Holy Spirit as seen in Galatians 5:22-23.

Reread: 1 Timothy 6:11

Conversely, what things does Paul tell Timothy to pursue? Again, please make a list.

1.

2.

3.

4.

5.

6.

Are we to also pursue these things? How so?

Do you regard the things on this second list to be the opposite of the items from which we are to flee?

When we flee from the destructive things on the first list we reviewed today and to the constructive things on the second list it has an impact upon us. How would you describe that impact?

What impact does it have upon other believers when we proceed as noted on these two lists?

What impact does it have upon unbelievers when we follow this pattern?

Thinking of this in reverse, how does it impact both other believers and unbelievers when we do not follow God's prescribed pattern for our lives as put forth in these two lists?

Note: The gentleness mentioned in the second list is correctly understood to be the concept spoken of in 2 Timothy 1:7. It is not weakness or timidity.

How would you describe this quality in your own words having read 2 Timothy 1:7?

Reread: 1 Timothy 6:12

Note: The Greek word translated to "fight" (1 Timothy 6:12 NLT) in English is *agone*, from which we get the English word "agony." The Greek indicates a struggle and straining to win. We see this same concept in:

2 Timothy 4:7.

1 Corinthians 9:25-27.

What fight did Paul tell Timothy to take part in?

Considering what was happening in Ephesus at the time, what do you take this to mean?

What does this mean to you in the world today?

How does it apply to you personally?

To what did Paul tell Timothy to hold tight?

What had Timothy done so far with the possession Paul encouraged him to hold on to so tightly?

What is the significance of Timothy having held onto this possession in front of so many witnesses?

How might this apply to believers today? Please explain.

Reread: 1 Timothy 6:13

Note: Dictionaries define the word "charge" (1 Timothy 6:13 NLT) with this usage as "a demand as a price from someone for services rendered or goods supplied."

What do you take the charge given by Paul to Timothy to mean in the context of this verse?

In whose sight did Paul charge Timothy?

Before whom did Jesus Christ make what Paul refers to as His "good confession" (1 Timothy 4:1 NLT)?

Read John 18:28-37 to see what Paul was referring to as the 'good confession" (1 Timothy 4:1 NLT), of Jesus Christ.

Before whom have you made a confession of your faith?

Reread: 1 Timothy 6:13-14

With what command did Paul charge Timothy?

For how long was Timothy to adhere to this charge?

Note: The Greek word translated "appearance" (1 Timothy 3:14 BSV) is *epiphaneia* which is literally translated epiphany in English. This is defined as an appearance or manifestation of a deity and is also used to denote a special moment of revelation or insight. In Christendom it is the term applied to a festival by the same name to commemorate when Jesus as an infant appeared before the Gentiles visiting from the east. (There is a much more to this event as a good student of history and the Scriptures can find. See *Dynamic Studies in John* for an explanation of this.) In the context of 1 Timothy 6:14 it refers to the second coming of Jesus before not only the Jews but also the Gentiles at a future point in time known as the end of The Great Tribulation.

In what fashion was Timothy to obey this charge? What were the two primary qualifiers or descriptors of his conduct to be?

1.

2.

What does this mean to you in practical terms?

Reread: 1 Timothy 6:15

When, according to these verses, will Jesus Christ's "appearing" (1 Timothy 6:15 GNT) take place in the broad span of human history?

What titles do we see applied to Jesus in these verses?

1.

2.

3.

Where else do we see these titles in the whole of Scripture?

Read the following verses for help:

Deuteronomy 10:17

Psalm 136:3

Daniel 2:47

Revelation 1:5

Revelation 17:14

Revelation 19:16

What do you make of this?

Reread: 1 Timothy 6:16

What attributes of God the Father are listed in this verse?

1.

2.

3.

What is due to God the Father?

1.

2.

How long are these things due to Him?

Read:

Exodus 33:20

John 1:18

John 5:37

1 John 4:12

Romans 1:20

Hebrews 11:27

Colossians 1:15-18

Colossians 2:9-10

1 Timothy 1:17

How do these verses relate to Jesus Christ and/or God the Father?

How do the attributes of God influence your worship of Him?

Reread: 1 Timothy 6:17

What are people who are rich in the things of this world to not do?

1.

2.

Why are they to not do this?

What impact does it have upon those who are rich, other believers and nonbelievers if those who are rich engage in the behaviors specifically warned against in this verse?

Why is it easy for people to trust in their possessions, accomplishments or abilities?

Conversely, what are those who are rich in the things of this world commanded to do?

What is the promised result for people who put their hope in God?

Note: The use of the word "hope" in the Greek is the opposite of our use of the word in English. In the Greek, "hope" is a confidence, sureness and knowledge of future things. In fact, in the Greek, the word "hope" infers a certainty stronger than knowing. It is an ultimate, internal, overpowering, all-enveloping eternal surety and truth that is absolute.

Understanding the import of this concept, what does this mean to you in practical terms as you live your life?

Additional Note: It has been pointed out by Dr. Charles Missler that one of the greatest dangers of wealth is that it tends to make a person proud. Such a person then understands neither themselves nor their wealth. See the following verses and discuss any further insights you gain into the proper view and utilization of wealth:

Deuteronomy 8:18

Joshua 1:8

Reread: 1 Timothy 6:18

What practical commands does God give those who are rich in this world's eyes to follow?

1.

2.

3.

4.

Reread: 1 Timothy 6:19

Also read:

Matthew 6:33

Matthew 6:19-21

Luke 12:19-21

John 10:10

What two results will those who follow the commands in 1 Timothy 6:18 see?

Why do you think the proper use of one's wealth is tied to their ability to experience true life through Jesus?

How can a person "lay up treasures in heaven" (Matthew 6:20 KJV)?

Reread: 1 Timothy 6:20-21

What was Timothy to guard?

Should we be doing the same? How so?

What was Timothy to turn away from?

1.

2.

If Timothy was to turn away from these things it implies that he was faced with them. What kind of godless chatter and weird ideas that some falsely call knowledge are believers faced with in the world today?

Should we then respond to such inaccuracies, pseudo-scholarship and destructive thinking in the same way as Timothy?

What has been the result over history when people have gotten off the track and fallen prey to false ideas and teaching?

Note: Correctly avoiding destructive and inaccurate philosophies, statements and teaching is not a matter of chance. Believers need to arm themselves appropriately. For more insight into this see *How to Avoid Error* in the appendices of this book.

How does Paul conclude his letter to Timothy?

Note:

Grace is defined as getting what you don't deserve.

Mercy is defined as not getting what you do.

One of the great legal minds and students of history of the past two thousand years was John Selden who lived in England from 1584 until his death in 1654. His personal library alone held over 8,000 volumes. Upon his death bed he is reported to have said: "I have surveyed much of the learning that is among the sons of men, and my study is filled with books and manuscripts on various subjects. But at present, I cannot recollect any passage out of all my books and papers whereon I can rest my soul, save this from the sacred Scriptures: "The grace of God that bringeth salvation hath appeared to all men" (Titus 2:11 KJV)."

How does this final recorded statement of this learned man impact you?

What do you think Paul intended for Timothy to understand by concluding his letter as he did?

Application Questions

How can you fight the good fight of faith each day?

What preventative measures can you take each day to be sure that you don't begin to wander from the faith?

What steps can you take to incorporate the qualities Paul told Timothy to pursue in your life this week?

What specific actions can you take to store up treasure in heaven?

Close in Prayer

INTRODUCTION TO PAUL'S SECOND LETTER TO TIMOTHY

Prior to examining and analyzing this letter we would do well to make a quick summary review of Paul's life. This is presented below in a roughly chronological order. Because he was so active this summary will likely leave out activities of consequence that you feel should be included. Please feel free to add them to the list.

1. Saul, who would later be called Paul, was perhaps the most intelligent and highly educated man of his time.

2. He was a Jew.

3. He encouraged and participated in the persecution, imprisonment, and murder of those who followed Jesus.

4. The same Jesus whom he attacked appeared before him on the road to Damascus and Paul subsequently became a follower of Jesus Christ, Yeshua Ha-Maschiach, the Jewish Messiah.

5. He spent the next three years in the Arabian desert.

6. He was forced to escape from Damascus in a basket lowered from the city walls.

7. He spent about ten years in Tarsus.

8. Barnabas brought him to Antioch.

9. He went on to what is often called his first missionary journey to spread the Good News of life through Jesus.

10. He participated in the Council in Jerusalem where the momentous decision was made to purposely carry the Good News about the Jewish Messiah and life through him to the Gentiles.

11. He subsequently took what is termed his second missionary journey.

12. He was joined in his efforts by Timothy.

13. He then undertook what is called his third missionary journey.

14. He was arrested in Judea approximately ten years before this letter was written.

15. He was imprisoned in Caesarea for two years.

16. When on trial he invoked his right as a Roman citizen to appeal to Caesar.

17. After invoking this right he was sent to Rome on a ship.

18. The ship on which he was traveling was wrecked at sea and he spent about three months on Malta.

19. He was placed on house arrest in Rome.

20. The book of Acts was likely the document prepared as a summary for the court in Rome to be read prior to his trial.

21. He wrote the "prison epistles" which we know as Ephesians, Philippians and Colossians.

22. He was acquitted of the charges against him and released.

23. When in Macedonia he wrote 1st Timothy and Titus.

24. He was arrested again and put in a dungeon from which he wrote 2nd Timothy, which appears to have been his last letter.

We should also point out that there are a number of good books about the life of Paul that might be helpful to read for anyone wishing to know more about this amazing man. Perhaps the best is *A Jew from Tarsus* by Dr. Steve White.

As this letter opens we should realize:

1. It is now 67 years after the birth of Jesus.

2. Paul has been rearrested and is now imprisoned in Rome.

3. This time he is in chains. See 2 Timothy 1:16.

4. The treatment he is receiving is that of a criminal with no sanitation and little light. See 2 Timothy 2:9.

5. He has had one trial at which he was abandoned. See 2 Timothy 4:16.

6. He appears to bear no animosity toward those who have abandoned him in his last days on earth.

7. He preached the Gospel at his trial. See 2 Timothy 4:17.

8. Prior to his arrest he had been traveling.

9. He forgot his cloak, books and papers at Troas. See 2 Timothy 4:13.

10. He visited Corinth and Miletus, leaving friends in both places. See 2 Timothy 4:20.

11. He also may have again visited Ephesus where there had been extreme trouble for and persecution of believers with more yet to come. See 2 Timothy 4:14-15.

12. This seems to be Paul's final letter.

13. Though he is expecting to be executed soon, he is writing to encourage his close friend Timothy. See 2 Timothy 2:1

14. Paul was reportedly beheaded for his faith in Rome the year after this letter was written.

15. This letter, therefore, takes on the role of a deathbed communication.

16. Such deathbed communications are generally given more weight than casual letters of communication and conversation.

This then raises two important questions for each of us to answer.

1. What would the most intelligent, well-read, man of the first century AD say to his best friend when this well-educated man knew he was about to be executed? This we will see in our study of the second letter to Timothy and we would all do well to take careful note of it. If it applied to Timothy it most certainly applies to us. In more contemporary terms we might regard it as a letter from Alfred Einstein to each of us on a personal basis in regard to the human intelligence behind it. Realizing that it is also part of what we know to be the inspired and inerrant Word of God meant for each of us on a personal basis, we should regard it with even greater respect and an eagerness to learn and apply the truths contained therein.

2. What do you wish to impart if you have the opportunity to prepare a written last communique to those you love before you die? What will you say and what will you discuss? Please make a list remembering that this will be your last list.

1.

2.

3.

4.

5.

6.

7.

WEEK 9

BE FAITHFUL
2 TIMOTHY 1:1-2:13

Open in Prayer

Note: This letter is essentially Paul's "deathbed" communication and is light years away from some religious organizations today described by Chuck Missler as "a church made up of a mild-mannered man standing before a group of mild-mannered people, urging them to be more mild-mannered." Nothing could be further from the vitality and life to be found in God's Word, which we call the Bible.

Group Warm-Up Questions

What is characteristic of the people you enjoy being around?

In what ways have your parents or grandparents significantly shaped your life?

Read: 2 Timothy 1:1-2:13

Reread: 2 Timothy 1:1

For what did Paul say he was chosen and appointed?

Reread: 2 Timothy 1:2

How did Paul regard Timothy?

What was Paul's wish for Timothy?

Reread: 2 Timothy 1:3

What did Paul do day and night?

What do you think Paul meant when he said that he and his ancestors both served God with a clear conscience?

Do you serve God with a clear conscience? How so?

Is it possible that a person might be serving God but without a clear conscience?

What ought someone to do if they are serving God without a clear conscience? Read the following verses as you construct your answer.

Proverbs 28:13

Leviticus 5:5

Hebrews 12:1

Psalm 32:1-11

James 5:16

Mark 11:25

James 4:7-10

1 John 1:9

2 Timothy 3:16-17

1 Thessalonians 5:16-22

Note: It is clear that Paul's prayers were not routine and rote. How can we be sure our prayers also do not become routine?

Reread: 2 Timothy 1:4

Why did Paul long to see Timothy again?

What did Paul expect to be the result of a reunion with Timothy if in fact they were able to have one?

When have you been refreshed by another believer? Please explain.

If Paul and Timothy were not able to arrange such a reunion in this life, what was Paul's expectation for such a reunion in the next?

With whom do you hope to have such a reunion while still on this earth?

With whom do you look forward to such a reunion after the first death?

Note: It is said that those who have trusted Jesus die once and live twice while those who do not live once and die twice. How might you describe this to someone?

Reread: 2 Timothy 1:5

Who were Eunice and Lois?

What did Timothy share with them?

How do you think the faith of Timothy's mother and grandmother influenced him?

How did Paul characterize the faith of these three people?

What family member or friend has had the greatest role in your spiritual development?

Reread: 2 Timothy 1:6

What did Paul remind Timothy to do?

Must we also do this same thing on a daily basis?

How can we effectively do so?

Read the following verses as you construct your answer.

Matthew 4:4

1 Thessalonians 5:17

Hebrews 10:25

Ephesians 5:18-20

What gift has God given you? (Everybody has at least one.)

Reread: 2 Timothy 1:7

What two things are decidedly not from God's Spirit?

1.

2.

What three things are most definitely from the Holy Spirit?

1.

2.

3.

How do you see these things showing up in your life?

Reread: 2 Timothy 1:8

Have you ever felt ashamed about something you believe? How so?

About whom and what should believers never be ashamed?

In what way can believers be ready when suffering comes their way?

Why does suffering come the way of believers?

Have you suffered for the sake of the Good News? How so?

Read:

John 15:18

John 16:33

What do we learn about suffering and persecution from these verses?

What do we learn about inner peace and victory?

Reread: 2 Timothy 1:9

Also read: Ephesians 1:4

To what did God call us when we received new life through the sacrifice of Jesus?

When did He come up with this plan?

Why did God bless believers with this new life?

Is this new life a component in the suffering that is experienced by believers? Please explain how you have seen this working in real time.

Despite this suffering, are believers still victorious?

Read the following verses as you put together your answer.

Romans 8:35-37

2 Corinthians 4:8

Romans 8:28

Philippians 4:6-7

Romans 5:3-5

Psalm 34:19

Joshua 1:9

James 1:12

Jeremiah 29:11

Isaiah 40:31

Galatians 6:9

Reread: 2 Timothy 1:10

How has all of this been made plain to us?

Also read:

2 Timothy 1:10 again.

John 14:6

John 3:16

John 10:10

What things, specifically, did Jesus accomplish as mentioned in these verses?

1.

2.

3.

Reread: 2 Timothy 1:11-12

For what did God choose Paul?

Why was Paul suffering as a result of what God appointed him to do?

Read: Romans 1:16

Why was Paul not ashamed in the least for doing what God had chosen him for?

Reread: 2 Timothy 1:12

How does the assuredness Paul had relate to every person who has trusted Jesus on a personal basis?

How, most specifically, does this assurance relate to you on a personal and daily basis?

Can you think of a time when this assurance has impacted you in a positive and supportive fashion in your life? Please explain?

Reread: 2 Timothy 1:13

What did Paul instruct Timothy to do in regard to the wholesome teaching he had received?

How had this wholesome teaching been shaped?

What or whose pattern of sound teaching are you following?

Reread: 2 Timothy 1:14

By what power was Timothy to hold on to the precious truth that had been imparted to him?

Why do you think Paul tells Timothy to guard this truth?

Read the following verses as you put together your answer.

2 Timothy 2:16

2 Timothy 2:23-24

Titus 3:9

Hebrews 4:14-15

1 Corinthians 10:13

2 Timothy 1:7

Reread: 2 Timothy 1:15

Who had abandoned Paul when he was imprisoned this time around?

Do you think these two people were also overtly rejecting Jesus Christ?

How do think these two people might feel and fare when they stand before God on judgment day having been singled out over thousands of years for deserting Paul when he was imprisoned for his faith? Read the following verses as you think about this question.

Matthew 10:33

John 12:48

1 John 2:23

When have you felt abandoned by a friend?

Note: It is of interest to realize that Paul spent three years in Ephesus, the capital of Asia. When he was there he evangelized the entire region with all seven of the major groups of believers (churches) being addressed in the book of Revelation.

Reread: 2 Timothy 1:15-18

What do we learn about Onesiphorus and his family?

1.

2.

3.

4.

5.

6.

7.

Why do you think Onesiphorus and his family acted as they did while everyone else acted in a cowardly manner? Please revisit 2 Timothy 1:7 for clues as you construct your answer.

Can you think of a time when something like this happened to you? Please explain?

Note: Some researchers think that Onesiphorus was also arrested and persecuted for his faith and his continued support of Paul. They point to 2 Timothy 4:19 where we see that others were, at that time, occupying his household. Someday in the future we will know for sure.

Reread: 2 Timothy 2:1

What does Paul again tell Timothy to do?

Do you think this is a command or just some nice suggestion?

Are we to also do this? How so?

Note: We should realize that having been involved with Paul at Ephesus, Timothy already had available to him Ephesians 6:10-18 with specific instructions on how to be strong.

Why do you think Paul gave him this further reminder in his second letter to him?

Do we also need to be reminded about how to access God's power and to be strong? How so?

Can periodically reviewing and/or memorizing passages of Scripture like Ephesians 6:10-18 aid us in this endeavor? How does this work in a person's life?

Reread: 2 Timothy 2:2

What had Timothy heard Paul do?

If the things Timothy heard Paul teach were confirmed by many witnesses, to what do you think he was referring?

Remember there were still many people around that had:

1. Seen Jesus when He walked the earth.

2. Seen Jesus when He was resurrected.

3. Known people who had seen and heard Jesus when He walked the earth or when He was raised from death.

It was just not good form or even thought to be intelligent to doubt the reality of these things at this point in time in the world in which they lived.

How do you think this may or may not be similar to:

1. The way in which the general populace in the world thought and spoke of the Holocaust thirty years after it occurred?

2. The way in which the general populace of the world thinks about the Holocaust nearly 100 years after its occurrence?

Why do you think this is so?

Read: Hebrews 4:12

What part does the Word of God play in proper teaching?

Reread: 2 Timothy 2:3

What else does Paul tell Timothy to do?

What do you think he meant by this in practical terms?

How does this apply to believers today?

When and how have you suffered for or because of the Gospel?

Reread: 2 Timothy 2:4

What do good soldiers not do?

Why do they not do this?

Reread: 2 Timothy 2:5

Also read:

Philippians 3:14

1 Corinthians 9:24-25

What can stop even good athletes from winning "the prize?"

Reread: 2 Timothy 2:6

Also read: Proverbs 24:30-34

What should hardworking farmers be able to do?

Reread:

2 Timothy 2:3-6

2 Timothy 2:7

Also read:

1 Corinthians 9:7

1 Timothy 5:18

What truths do you understand from these verses?

1.

2.

3.

4.

5.

6.

7.

Reread: 2 Timothy 2:8

Also read: John 14:19

What is the essence of the Good News?

Reread: 2 Timothy 2:9

Why was Paul chained like a dog?

What cannot be chained?

How does the fact that the Word of God cannot be chained impact people around the world?

Reread: 2 Timothy 2:10

For what is Paul willing to endure anything?

Why did he feel so strongly about this?

How do you feel about this?

Reread: 2 Timothy 2:11-13

These verses contain several statements that have a direct result in one's life. They are presented in an if/then fashion. Please dissect these verses noting each combination and then note what they mean.

Statement 1

If:

Then:

What this means:

Statement 2

If:

Then:

What this means:

Statement 3

If:

Then:

What this means:

Statement 4

If:

Then:

What this means:

Reread: 2 Timothy 2:11

In God's Word there are a very few statements that are characterized as "trustworthy or faithful sayings." Besides 2 Timothy 2:11 (NLT, NIV, ESV, BSV, KJV, NKJV, etc.) they include:

1 Timothy 1:15 (NLT, NIV, ESV, BSV, KJV, NKJV, etc.)

1 Timothy 4:8-9 (NLT, NIV, ESV, BSV, KJV, NKJV, etc.)

Titus 3:7-8 (NLT, NIV, ESV, BSV, KJV, NKJV, etc.)

In 1 John 5:4 we see that it is Jesus Himself who gives us the victory.

Reread: 2 Timothy 2:12

Note: Based upon this verse, some scholars such as J. Vernon McGee, Joseph Dillow and others believe this verse indicates that not all believers are going to reign with Him, but only those who have suffered for Him. This, of course, begs the question of "What degree of difficulty comprises such suffering?"

What are your thoughts about this?

Reread: 2 Timothy 2:13

How should God's faithfulness impact our commitment to Him and His Messiah? Why?

Application Questions

What person who has had a substantial impact on your spiritual life will you take the time to thank personally this week?

How can you refresh another believer this week?

Who is someone for whom you can commit to pray on a regular basis?

Close in Prayer

WEEK 10

AN APPROVED WORKER
2 TIMOTHY 2:14-26

Open in Prayer

Group Warm-Up Questions

When was the last really stupid argument you had with someone?

Whose approval did you seek most as a teenager?

When was the last time you felt thoroughly embarrassed?

Read: 2 Timothy 2:14-26

Reread: 2 Timothy 2:14

Remember: This letter is the last one from Paul, perhaps the most highly-educated, well read, and intelligent man of his time, to his protégé'. It is, as we said previously, essentially his death bed testament as he was soon to be executed and he knew it. Within it he passes along things that he felt were of great importance.

With this as a backdrop, why do you think Paul commands, actually commands and not suggests that Timothy follow what he tells him in this verse?

What results from quarreling over words?

How can stupid and useless arguments ruin those who hear them? How does this work?

About what sorts of things can believers get into senseless arguments with other believers if they are not careful?

Have you ever seen this happen? Please explain if you have.

Read:

1 Timothy 6:4

Titus 3:9

What additional insight do these verses give us into the concept Paul is discussing in 2 Timothy 2:14?

Why does God's Word repeatedly warn us against such things?

Reread: 2 Timothy 2:15

How does Paul encourage Timothy to present himself before God?

What are some of the aspects of this successful presentation as noted in this verse?

1.

2.

3.

4.

Putting it into your own words, what do you think it means to be approved by God?

What kinds of circumstances make you feel ashamed or embarrassed? Please explain?

How can we please God with our work?

Reread: 2 Timothy 2:16

What does Paul tell Timothy to avoid? (You may want to read this verse in several translations to get the full flavor of it.)

What is the significance of the way Paul describes this type of thing?

To what does engaging in the practice Paul warns against lead?

Why do you think this is so considering the way human beings are put together?

When are you tempted to engage in godless chatter or stupid arguments?

Chuck Missler says that "even Bible-babble" can prove vapid unless applied to the real world." What do you think he means by this?

Do you think he is right or wrong? How so?

Reread: 2 Timothy 2:17

Note: The Merriam Webster dictionary defines a canker as an "erosive or spreading sore." The concept is also often associated with gangrene. Some versions of the Bible define the physical manifestation of the problem addressed in the verse as a spreading "cancer" (NLT, NKJV).

What can happen when this type of thing begins to take place?

Why, in your opinion, is this so often true?

Paul goes to great lengths to let us know how destructive this type of talk can be. Why do you think he hits this topic so hard?

What two people does Paul single out as being guilty of this destructive practice?

How would you feel if your legacy as communicated to billions of people over thousands of years was that of Hymenaeus and Philetus?

Note: Hymenaeus and Philetus were involved with the early church in Ephesus. They were prominent examples of false teachers who had purposely strayed from sound Biblical teaching for their own gain. They and another of their compatriots are mentioned in the letters to Timothy. See:

1. 2 Timothy 2:17 where Philetus and Hymenaeus mentioned as false teachers leading some people away from faith.

2. 1 Timothy 1:18-20 where Hymenaeus is mentioned in league with Alexander as false teachers who have violated their consciences.

3. 2 Timothy 4:14-16 where we again see an Alexander, widely believed to be the same Alexander mentioned in Paul's first letter to Timothy, as doing much harm to Paul and the message of the Scriptures.

4. Romans 8:5-9 where we see an expansion of the problem evidenced in the lives of Philetus, Hymenaeus and Alexander.

5. 1 Corinthians 5:1-5 where we see Paul dealing with another situation of overt disobedience destructive to the fellowship of believers.

Further Note: For the health of the body of believers we see some of the false teachers and trouble makers mentioned in these verses thrown out of the fellowship. See:

1. 1 Timothy 1:19-20. Interestingly, the term for what Hymenaeus and Alexander have done with their faith is a nautical term and means "thrown overboard."

2. 1 Corinthians 5:5.

While we do not have enough information about these particular trouble makers to make further comments on their specific situation we do know that they were either:

1. Pretenders who had wormed their way into the fellowship for personal gain and were exposed for what they were.

2. Extremely misled and confused believers ultimately disciplined by God. (Hebrews 12:6) This second possibility seems quite unlikely since we see no evidence of it by the measure of the objective standard we see in the Scriptures emanating from the lives of those following God and being guided by His Holy Spirit.

How would you like to be remembered?

What can you do today and on an ongoing basis to be remembered as you desire?

Reread: 2 Timothy 2:17-18

What specific lie did Hymenaeus and Philetus spread?

Note: This was not the last time this lie was encountered. Indeed, we see an entire chapter of 2 Thessalonians devoted to this tactic from the enemy. In order to understand what was going on and still sometimes goes on in the world today I suggest everyone take a 5 minute break and read:

2 Thessalonians 2:1-17

Reread: 2 Timothy 2:17-18

What was the result of Hymenaeus and Philetus spreading this untruth?

How could they have possibly succeeded when spreading such an obvious falsehood?

Why did it work with some people?

Do we see things like this happening in the world today? Please explain?

What false doctrines have destroyed the faith, such as it was, of someone you know? Why do you think this happened?

Reread: 2 Timothy 2:19

This is translated in the NKJV as:

"Nevertheless the solid foundation of God stands, having this seal: "The Lord knows those who are His," and, "Let everyone who names the name of Christ depart from iniquity.""

The NLT says it:

"But God's truth stands firm like a foundation stone with this inscription: "The Lord knows those who are his," and "All who belong to the Lord must turn away from evil.""

The importance of adhering to God's standards is not a new concept. We find it throughout God's Word. We see a few examples of this in:

- Matthew 7:23.

- Psalm 6:8.

- Luke 13:27.

Furthermore, the Cambridge dictionary defines a foundation stone as:

- "a large block of stone that is put in position at the start of work on a public building, often with a ceremony."

or

- "the basic or important principles, ideas, facts, etc. on which something depends:

  Freedom of speech is the foundation stone of democracy."

What stands like a foundation stone?

Read: 2 Timothy 3:16-17

Also read: Deuteronomy 6:6-9

Wherein do we find this truth?

Note: Abu Ali ibn al-Haytham, the natural philosopher of 11th century Iraq and the founder of the scientific method in the east said:

"The seeker after truth (his beautiful description of the scientist) does not place his faith in any mere consensus, however venerable or widespread. Instead, he subjects what he has learned of it to inquiry, inspection and investigation. The road to the truth is long and hard, but it is the road we must follow."

(Quoted by Gregory Wrightstone in Inconvenient Facts, page 80, published by Silver Crown production in 2017.)

Read: Acts 17:11

How might you relate what Abu Ali ibn al-Haytham said to the Word of God?

How is it that God's Word acts like a foundation stone?

What two part inscription does Peter say would appear on a foundation stone derived of God's Word? Please enumerate the two parts and put them in your own words.

1.

2.

How is it that the Lord knows those who are His regardless of the opinion of those in the world?

Why is it imperative that those who are His must turn away from evil?

Read:

Galatians 6:5

Philippians 1:11

1 Thessalonians 4:1

Colossians 3:23-24

Colossians 4:5-6

Philippians 2:12-13

Philippians 2:14-16

Ephesians 6:5-8

1 Peter 2:20

1 Peter 3:12-17

Matthew 10:33

Luke 12:9

2 Timothy 1:7-8

1 Peter 4:16

1 Peter 4:11

Philippians 1:27

1 Corinthians 10:31

Colossians 3:17

Colossians 3:23-24 (Again.)

Does this imply that some of those who have become "His" may have been engaged in some activities that they needed to turn away from?

If that is the case, what should now characterize their lives?

Reread: 2 Timothy 2:20

Note: This is an obvious use of allegory in Scripture. It is quite different from the way some modern "theologians" contrive to bend Scripture to their own ends by claiming allegory where none exists.

What kinds of utensils are found in a wealthy home?

What are the expensive utensils used for?

To what use are the cheap utensils put?

What does it mean to you that believers are referred to as "utensils" (NLT)?

Reread: 2 Timothy 2:21

What are the characteristics of those who keep themselves pure?

1.

2.

3.

Conversely, what are the characteristics of those who do not keep themselves pure?

How can we cleanse ourselves from insignificant pursuits?

How can we strike a balance that is acceptable to God when engaging in things that we enjoy that are not counter to God's standard as put forth in His Word? Please explain.

Can God, in fact, use our personal interests or hobbies in a way that is pleasing to Him? How so?

Reread: 2 Timothy 2:22

From what does Paul tell Timothy to run?

Note: Those who have trusted God have often had to flee from doing what is wrong for thousands of years. For an example of this see Genesis 39: 6-12 written at least 3,500 years ago.

What does Paul tell Timothy to pursue?

1.

2.

3.

4.

5.

What desires of youth might tempt us?

Paul specifically tells Timothy to associate with those who call upon the Lord with pure hearts. Do you think this means that he is also telling him to stay away from those who call upon the Lord with impure hearts? How so?

Please read the following verses as you put together your answer.

Proverbs 13:20

1 Corinthians 15:33

Psalm 1:1

Proverbs 14:7

Psalm 26:4-5

1 Corinthians 5:6-12

How does this relate to us today?

Reread: 2 Timothy 2:23

What does Paul tell Timothy to stay away from?

Why does he tell him to do this?

How would you characterize the kinds of arguments Paul tells Timothy to avoid?

Please provide a contemporary example from your experience.

Reread: 2 Timothy 2:24

In general, what qualities should characterize a servant of the Lord?

1.

2.

3.

4.

Reread: 2 Timothy 2:25

Also read: Colossians 4:5-6

How is a servant of the Lord to instruct those who are in error about the clear truths of Scripture?

Can you think of a time when this admonition was correctly applied? What was the result? Please explain.

Can you think of a time when this was incorrectly done? What happened?

Reread: 2 Timothy 2:26

Also read: Romans 12:2

How would you describe the way in which people who oppose the truth are held captive?

What can happen when someone's heart and mind are changed by God?

Did this happen to you? Please explain.

Can you think of a time when you have seen this happen to someone else? How so?

Note: We have been discussing a portion of Paul's advice to Timothy. This also applies to us. However, we must also remember that this is only part of the story. We must never rely on "one verse or even one passage theology." In fact, we must not ever rely upon a topical summary in which Scriptural references are "cherry picked" or even distorted to support a particular point of view. We must see and understand God's Word and plan as a whole. (See *How to Avoid Error* in the appendices of this book.)

Application Questions

What can you do to present yourself as one approved by God?

How do you need to change your daily speech to weed out senseless and godless chatter?

What can you do to flee temptation?

Close in Prayer

WEEK 11

THE LAST DAYS
2 TIMOTHY 3:1-9

Open in Prayer

Group Warm-Up Questions

What adjectives would you use to describe the world in which we live today?

What goals drive the people with whom you work and live?

Read: 2 Timothy 3:1-9

Reread: 2 Timothy 3:1

To what did Paul call our attention?

How did Paul characterize this period of time?

Note: To gain a true understanding of these times we should realize that:

1. The same word used to describe these times in 2 Timothy 3:1 is used to describe the demoniacs in Matthew 8:28-34. Please read these verses to bring this home.

2. Looking at this in concert with 1 Timothy 4:1 seems to indicate even more. Please discuss what you see as the implications of this.

3. Taking this one step further we see in Acts 20:29-30 that this began long ago.

4. Looking at Scripture as a whole we see this same terminology regarding "the last days (2 Peter 3:3-4 EST and 1 Peter 1:20 NLT), the time of the end (Daniel 8:17; 12:4 NLT and Daniel 8:19 NIV and ESV), and the end of the age (Matthew 13:39, 40, 49 GNB)" as referring to the times both preceding the event known as the Rapture (*harpazo*) and extending through the time known as the Great Tribulation.

Reread: 2 Timothy 3:2-5

Note: Please be sure to read this in the KJV as well as any other translations you may be using.

In these verses God has provided us with at least 19 indicators of the state of the hearts of people in the last days. Please list them.

1.

2.

3.

4.

5.

6.

7.

8.

9.

10.

11.

12.

13.

14.

15.

16.

17.

18.

19.

Looking at this list and the state of the world in general today, how would you answer those who claim that the world is getting better and better?

Note: Amazingly, there are books written today making the claim that human beings are becoming more loving, tolerant and kind. One, in particular, *The Better Angels of Our Nature* by Steven Pinker, employs an astounding use of non-sequiturs in an attempt to make this erroneous case. Today there are more wars, more people being martyred for their faith, more slavery of all types, more people being oppressed, more humans starving because of governmental manipulation, more examples of governmental and corporate corruption, and more instances of injustice in judicial systems than ever before in recorded history.

When studying the Scriptures, we are encouraged to follow the example of the Bereans as seen in Acts 17:11. They had been listening to Paul, possibly the most intelligent and educated man of their time and they were still checking up on him and what he said in relationship to the Scriptures to see if what he said was true. Please feel free to do the same and make an honest, intensive and thorough study of the claims in the above paragraph and see if you agree.

Do you feel that we are living in "The Last Days?" Why or why not?

Reread: 2 Timothy 3:2

In general, what will people be like during this period of time?

Reread: 2 Timothy 3:3

What will people in general lack during this time?

Reread: 2 Timothy 3:4

What will many people love instead of God?

Why is it so tempting to be a "lover of pleasure" (NIV, ESB, KJV, NKJV) rather than a lover of God?

Is there greater and more lasting pleasure available to those who love and follow God? Please read the following verses as you construct your answer.

Psalm 16

Proverbs 17:22

Psalm 147:11

1 Chronicles 29:17

Proverbs 15:13

Zephaniah 3:17

Proverbs 11:20

Proverbs 12:22

Ezekiel 33:11

Psalm 35:9

Psalm 111:2

Philippians 2:13

Ecclesiastes 2:4

1 Peter 4:3-4

John 10:10

Acts 17:10-11

Psalm 112:1

Psalm 37:4

Psalm 16:11

1 Timothy 6:17

Romans 7:22

Psalm 119:16

Jeremiah 15:16

Psalm 1:1-2

Reread: 2 Timothy 3:5

It may come as a surprise that despite the characteristic behavior of people in general at this time, many of them will be very religious. How does God describe the predominant religiosity of the time?

What are believers to do in relationship to people at this time who are falsely religious?

Does this command hold true at times besides those described as "near the end." How are we to then live, think and act? Please read the following references as you construct your answer.

1 Corinthians 15:33

1 Corinthians 5:11

Proverbs 13:20

Proverbs 14:7

Proverbs 25:26

Psalm 119:15

Psalm 26:4-5

Colossians 4:5-6

Ephesians 4:29-30

Ephesians 4:17

Romans 12:2

Joshua 1:8

Philippians 4:8

Proverbs 3:5-6

Psalm 1:1-4

Reread: 2 Timothy 3:6

What are some of the vilest characteristics of these people? Please list them:

1.

2.

Reread: 2 Timothy 3:7

What are the hallmarks of the people being taken advantage of in this fashion?

Why do you think people like this can never seem to find their way?

Have you seen examples of this in the world today? Please explain.

How might the application of 2 Timothy 3:16-17 be of assistance to them?

Reread: 2 Timothy 3:8

What are the two main characteristics of the false teachers described in the verses we are reviewing today?

1.

2.

What do you think it means that such people have depraved minds?

To what historical personages are these false teachers compared?

Note: Jannes and Jamres are the two magicians who opposed Moses and actually performed false miracles as recorded in Exodus 7 and 8. However, while their names are not specifically mentioned in the book of Exodus these two men were known historically.

Wayne Jackson writing in the Christian Courier said:

"The fact that the names of the magicians that opposed Moses are not recorded in the Old Testament does not mean that they were unknown.

Albert Pietersma has noted that the two names "appear frequently in Jewish, Christian, and pagan sources extant in Arabic, Aramaic, Greek, Hebrew, Latin

Old and Middle English, and Syriac" (*The Anchor Bible Dictionary*, ed. David Noel Freedman, New York: Doubleday, 1992, Vol. 3, p. 638).

Second Note: Jackson is referring to Luke 1:1-3 in his summary.

In what way does society encourage people to be controlled by evil desires?

Reread: 2 Timothy 3:9

How long will these false teachers get away with their evil schemes?

What will everyone eventually realize about them?

Here we note the use of the word "everyone" (2 Timothy 3:9 NIV, NLT, BSB, GNT). Do you think that this means that even the compatriots of these people will see them for what they are? Please explain.

Application Questions

From what ungodly person or group do you need to encourage other believers to disassociate themselves?

What specific negative attitude or behavior that is counter to God's standard will you ask God to help you overcome this week?

Close in Prayer

WEEK 12

FINAL CHARGE TO TIMOTHY
2 TIMOTHY 3:10-4:8

Open in Prayer

Group Warm-Up Questions

If the story of your life were made into a movie, what would the title be?

If you could be known for only one thing when you died, what would you want it to be?

Who is someone whose reputation you admire?

Read: 2 Timothy 3:10-4:8

Note: We would do well to remember that Paul was incarcerated in the Mamertime Prison in Rome at this writing and knew that his execution was near.

Reread: 2 Timothy 3:10-11

If Paul was married would not one expect that his wife would have known him better than anyone else?

However, it would appear that it was Timothy who knew Paul better than anyone else at this point in Paul's life.

Did Paul have a wife? Scripture seems to indicate that he did not at least at the point when he was writing. To partially clear up any questions, consider this:

1. Some people assume that Paul was married based upon 1 Corinthians 9:5. He was certainly affirming that workers such as he were free to have a believing wife accompany them on their travels and in their work.

2. However, looking at things globally, we find that he was not married at the time he wrote 1 Corinthians 7:1-7.

3. He was not married at the time he wrote 1 Corinthians 7:8-9.

4. It is possible, however, that he may have been married and widowed prior to the time he wrote to the Corinthians.

5. It is also possible that he may have been married after he wrote to the Corinthians.

6. Either way, his singleness at the time he wrote these letters is neither a universal pattern to follow nor prerequisite for service to God. Any statement to the contrary is simply not in concert with the Word of God.

Reread: 2 Timothy 3:10-11

What did Timothy know about Paul? Please make a list. (It is possible to break this down into 14 components.)

1.

2.

3.

4.

5.

6.

7.

8.

9.

10.

11.

12.

13.

14.

What sort of a reputation do you want to have?

What sort of a reputation DO you have at work, at school, or in your neighborhood?

Reread: 2 Timothy 3:11

For what did Paul say God rescued him?

Reread: 2 Timothy 3:12

What will happen to everyone who wants to live a godly life?

Can you think of times when you have seen this occur? Please explain.

Can you think of times when you were persecuted for wanting to live a godly life? What happened?

Note: Melvin R. Laird served as President Richard M. Nixon's first secretary of defense. In that position and related ones he faced many challenges and was embroiled in many controversies where he stood up for what he believed as he applied it to international and national politics. What most people don't know is that he appears to have been a dedicated Christian. He famously said "In this world it is becoming more and more unpopular to become a Christian. Soon it may become dangerous."

Interestingly, J. Vernon McGee, in his book *1 & 2 Timothy, Titus and Philemon* published by Thomas Nelson in 1995 said: "I believe that we are actually going to see the persecution of Christians in this country in the future. I do not mean the persecution of church members: the liberal church is so compromised today that they will go along with whatever comes along. I am saying that genuine believers in Christ may encounter persecution" (page 40).

What are your thoughts about what these two men said?

Paul C. Schenck with Robert Schenck published *The Extermination of Christianity: A Tyranny of Consensus* with Huntington House in 1993. In it he put forth what he referred to as "Five Steps of Persecution." A summarization of these steps might read:

1. Identify the target group.

2. Marginalize the target group.

3. Vilify the target group.

4. Pass laws against the beliefs or activities of the target group.

5. Enforce the laws.

In what ways do you see or not see this in action today as it relates to followers of Jesus Christ? Please give examples and explain.

Reread: 2 Timothy 3:13

What will evil men and imposters do? Again we are provided with a succinct summary list. Please enumerate.

1.

2.

3.

Do you imagine the life of evil men and imposters to be one of satisfaction?

How so?

Reread: 2 Timothy 3:14

What did Paul tell Timothy that Timothy must do?

What did Paul say that Timothy knew about the things he had been taught?

How, in general, did Timothy know about the people who taught him?

Reread: 2 Timothy 3:15

What was the primary source of the things Timothy had been taught?

For how long had he been studying this source?

What was the result of Timothy being taught by the Holy Scriptures?

Reread: 2 Timothy 3:16-17

Note: This is one of the most helpful short passages of Scripture and one that every believer ought to memorize. There is only truth and life for one who heeds the words contained in these verses.

Some people find it helpful to memorize John 3:16 in concert with these verses from Timothy. Besides the obvious citation similarities, why might these two references be so helpful when taken together?

Reread: 2 Timothy 3:16-17

What are the primary characteristics of Scripture? Please make this very important list.

1.

2.

3.

4.

5.

6.

7.

When finished, your list should include these concepts:

   1. All Scripture is inspired by God.

   2. It is useful for teaching the truth.

   3. It is useful for rebuking error.

   4. It is useful for correcting faults.

   5. It is useful for giving instructions for right living.

6. It enables the person who serves God to be fully qualified for every good work.

7. It equips the person who serves God to be equipped for every good work.

Knowing all of his, how should we use God's Word, the Bible, in our everyday lives?

How equipped are you for every good work?

Does your life demonstrate your faith? How so?

Reread: 2 Timothy 4:1

Who will Jesus Christ judge?

Reread: 2 Timothy 4:2

What specific things did Paul tell Timothy to do?

Please make a list.

1.

2.

3.

4.

5.

6.

7.

What was to be the basis of what Timothy said and did? (Hint: See 2 Timothy 3:16-17).

In what way should this also be the basis of what believers do today?

How can a person be sure God's Word is not only the guide for what they do but the crucible by which it is tested?

Reread: 2 Timothy 4:3

What time did Paul tell Timothy was coming?

Does this ever happen today? Please give an example.

Reread: 2 Timothy 4:4

What happens when people decide to reject sound teaching in favor of what is palatable?

What do you think are the results when people head in this direction?

Read: John 8:31-32

Also read: John 14:6

When people reject the truth to follow some other way, how does it impact their lives?

Read: Matthew 7:13-14

What are the further implications of this action in addition to the difficulties it brings into the lives of those who purposely choose the wrong path?

Reread: 2 Timothy 4:5

What four things in order did Paul tell Timothy to do?

1.

2.

3.

4.

Why is it so important that we, like Timothy, keep a clear mind as we follow the path God has laid before us?

What happens when we don't keep a clear mind?

What happens when we do keep a clear mind?

In what ways are all believers able to be good representatives of their Lord and to help others move toward trusting Him?

2 Timothy 4:6

Also read: Philippians 2:17

Note: Paul was a great biblical scholar. The concept of the drink offering which would be poured out over the sacrifice and disappear in steam was frequently mentioned in Exodus and Leviticus with which he was intimately familiar.

What did Paul know about his life?

What did he know about his death?

Reread: 2 Timothy 4:7

What else did Paul know about his life? What had he done?

1.

2.

3.

At the time of your death, do you believe you will be able to say these same things?

What can you do now to make sure that these three things will have characterized your life?

When you die, will it be more important that you can say these three crucial and primary things than the size of your final bank or investment account statement?

Are the two concepts in anyway intertwined? Please read the following verses as you contemplate and construct your answer.

Matthew 6:19-21

Luke 12:19-31

Matthew 25:35-40

Revelation 22:12

Proverbs 19:17

Colossians 3:1-3

Luke 12:15

Hebrews 6:10

Matthew 6:33

Romans 12:2

Note: In order to see this all work properly in one's life one must follow God's Word as a whole as so definitively and elegantly laid out for us. Please read the following verses and discuss how you see this all working together.

1 Corinthians 9:27

Hebrews 12:1-2

1 Corinthians 4:2

Reread: 2 Timothy 4:8

What prize awaited Paul?

When did he expect to receive it?

Who else will also receive this prize? Will you?

See the following verses as we realize that our final examination has already been scheduled:

Romans 14:12

Matthew 12:36

2 Corinthians 5:10

Isaiah 46:10

Job 14:5

Will you be ready?

Application Questions

How can you use the Bible in your own spiritual growth this week?

What can you do this week toward discharging all your duties?

Close in Prayer

PAUL'S FINAL COMMENTS
2 TIMOTHY 4:9-22

Open in Prayer

Group Warm-Up Questions

When have you felt abandoned by your friends?

What person would you like to visit whom you haven't seen in a while?

Read: 2 Timothy 4:9-22

Reread: 2 Timothy 4:9

What did Paul want Timothy to do?

Reread: 2 Timothy 4:10

What had Demas done?

Why had he done it?

What are your thoughts and feelings regarding what Paul had to say about Demas?

How would you feel if remembered in such a negative fashion for all time?

In what way are you tempted to "love the world?"

Is it sometimes more tempting to love the world than to love God? How so?

What things about the world to people naturally tend to love?

It is of particular interest that Paul is again alluding to this subject as he nears death. Why do you think this is so?

Please take a look at the following verses, which we did quite recently in a previous study, and jot down the additional insights you now have.

Matthew 6:19-21

Luke 12:19-31

Matthew 25:35-40

Revelation 22:12

Proverbs 19:17

Colossians 3:1-3

Luke 12:15

Hebrews 6:10

Matthew 6:33

Romans 12:2

How do you want to be remembered?

Reread: 2 Timothy 4:11

Who was with Paul?

Why did Paul want Timothy to bring Mark?

Reread: 2 Timothy 4:12

Whom did Paul send to Ephesus?

Note: Tychicus was somewhat famous in the New Testament world of believers. He was a faithful companion of Paul and Timothy. If there was a difficult job, Paul would often give the task to Tychicus. If a communique was to be delivered to embattled believers through enemy lines, he was the man who appeared to be able to get it done. We see him and his work mentioned in:

1. Acts 20:4 where he is numbered among those traveling with Paul during the time Paul was enduring plots against his life.

2. Ephesians 6:20-21 when Paul sent him into a difficult situation to deliver Paul's letter and to encourage the believers in the largest pagan city of its day.

3. Colossians 4:7 when Paul again sent him to deliver one of his communiques to beleaguered believers.

4. Titus 3:12 when he was mentioned along with Timothy as one of the two people Paul might send to Crete.

5. 2 Timothy 4:12 where Paul tells Timothy he had sent this good soldier and faithful brother to Ephesus.

6. Titus 3:12 when Paul was considering sending Tychicus or Artemas as trouble shooters to Crete to help Titus deal with a difficult situation.

Reread: 2 Timothy 4:13

What did Paul want Timothy to bring with him?

Why do you think he particularly wanted these things?

Note: Remember that Paul was perhaps the best read, most highly educated and intelligent man of his time. The aids to scholarship mentioned in this verse must have been quite important to him. It is of particular interest that his "books" (2 Timothy 4:13 NLT, NASB, ESV, GNT) were requested. The term he used in requesting his books was the Latin word *membranae,* which referred to a parchment notebook. This type of tool evolved into the *codex* or "book" that we have today. These bound parchments were very easy to handle, written on both sides of a sheet, often fit into a pocket, were easy to transport and store, and easy to use as references. They led to the ultimate demise of scrolls in daily use.

As strange as it may seem to some of us, the books we have been using for thousands of years are now, to some degree, being supplanted by the internet, MP3 and CD players, DVDs, podcasts, the radio and the like. Technologies like floppy discs are fading away, as are cassette players, although there seems to be resurgence in interest in vinyl records.

Reread: 2 Timothy 4:14

Also read: 1 Timothy 1:20

Who was Alexander?

What had he done to Paul?

What did Paul say would be the result in Alexander's life for what he had done?

What people today strongly oppose God's Word and the life-giving information contained in it? Why?

Read: 2 Timothy 4:1

How does this relate to you?

Knowing this, how ought we to live?

Reread: 2 Timothy 4:15

How did Paul instruct Timothy to deal with Alexander the Coppersmith?

How does this relate to how Paul had dealt with him earlier?

Reread: 2 Timothy 4:16

What happened at Paul's first defense?

How did Paul respond to their cowardly actions?

Why do some people seemingly abandon their faith or other believers at crucial points in life?

Did they ever have faith?

God's Word has some pretty pointed things to say about fear, cowardice, bravery, and courage.

To understand this properly, let's take a look at the definition of the words, emotions, and actions we are considering.

1. The Merriam Webster dictionary defines cowardice as "lack of courage or firmness of purpose."

2. It defines fear as "an unpleasant often strong emotion caused by anticipation or awareness of danger."

3. Conversely it defines courage as "mental or moral strength to venture, persevere, and withstand danger, fear, or difficulty."

4. It defines bravery as "the quality or state of having or showing mental or moral strength to face danger, fear, or difficulty."

Notice that courage and bravery are not necessarily the absence of fear, but the proper facing of it.

Nelson Mandela reportedly said "I learned that courage was not the absence of fear, but the triumph over it. The brave man is not he who does not feel afraid, but he who conquers that fear." If this seems familiar we should be aware that it is quite similar to what many courageous people have said over the centuries.

Let's take a look at the following biblical references and jot down what we learn about this in the Word of God:

Proverbs 28:1

Job 18:5-11

Matthew 10:28

Revelation 21:8

Matthew 10:33

1 John 4:18

Hebrews 13:5-6

Philippians 1:27

Deuteronomy 20:8

Deuteronomy 31:6

Proverbs 3:5-6

Proverbs 29:25

1 Corinthians 16:13

1 Corinthians 15:58

1 Chronicles 28:20

Ephesians 3:20

Philippians 4:13

Philippians 4:6

Romans 8:31

Joshua 1:9

Psalm 56:3-4

Isaiah 51:12

Isaiah 41:10-13

James 1:2-5

Psalm 31:24

Psalm 27:1

John 14:27

2 Timothy 1:7

Ephesians 6:10

Why do you think these concepts are so important in the Word of God and the life of a believer?

Reread: 2 Timothy 4:17

How did God deliver Paul when he was first brought before the judge?

1.

2.

What purposes were achieved when God delivered Paul in this fashion?

1.

2.

When has God delivered you from a hostile situation? What happened?

Reread: 2 Timothy 4:18

Of what was Paul convinced?

What exactly do you think he meant by this? Obviously it did not mean that Paul might not be executed or even tortured for his faith.

How is it possible that a believer might be victorious even when suffering, starving or dying for their faith?

Read the following verses as you put together your answer.

Romans 8:35-37

2 Corinthians 4:8

Romans 8:28

Philippians 4:6-7

Romans 5:3-5

Psalm 34:19

Joshua 1:9

James 1:12

Jeremiah 29:11

Isaiah 40:31

Galatians 6:9

Reread: 2 Timothy 4:19

Who did Paul send his greetings to?

Note: We have seen Priscilla and Aquila elsewhere in the New Testament documents. By piecing together what we have read we see:

1. Paul met them in Corinth after they had been expelled as refugees by Caesar along with all the other Jews.

    • See Acts 18:1-2.

2. They traveled with Paul when he left Corinth.

   • See Acts 18:18.

3. They were active in Ephesus where they helped Apollos better understand the Word of God.

   • See Acts 18:24-26

4. Paul sent special greetings to this special couple when he wrote Romans.

   • See Romans 16:3.

Reread: 2 Timothy 4:20

What did Paul say about Erastus and Trophimus?

Reread: 2 Timothy 4:21

When did Paul want Timothy to come and see him?

What other believers were encouraging and supporting Paul during his final hours?

Reread: 2 Timothy 4:22

Despite the fact that Paul was expecting to be executed momentarily, how did he end his letter to Timothy?

Why do you think he ended his letter in this fashion?

How would you feel if a friend about to be executed closed his final letter to you the way Paul closed this one to Timothy?

Application Questions

To what fellow believer can you show support this week? How?

How can you help a leader who is a believer with his or her efforts on behalf of the faith?

What comfort or encouragement can you provide to a person who is battling for the faith in a hostile setting?

Close in Prayer

INTRODUCTION TO TITUS

At the close of his last letter to Timothy, Paul recognized a number of the good and faithful soldiers in the faith. Among them was Tychicus with whom he entrusted the personal delivery of his letters through "enemy territory."

In the letter to Titus we find him addressing yet another of the faithful followers of the Jewish Messiah. In the case of Titus we would do well to recognize his resume' from Scripture itself. Here we find:

1. He was traveling with Paul and Barnabas to Jerusalem.

    •   See Galatians 2:1.

2. He assisted Paul in reviewing his work and message with the Jewish believers considered to be the leaders in the early church. It was Paul's goal to be sure that the message he was preaching was in concert with the then existent Scriptures (which we call the Old Testament or the Tanakh) and the message about them emanating from those in Jerusalem.

- See Galatians 2:2.

3. He was a Gentile from Greece who the Jewish believers accepted on the basis of his commitment to Jesus and not on the external ceremony of circumcision.

    - See Galatians 2:3.

4. He originally became a follower if Jesus Christ as a result of personal interaction with Paul.

    - See Titus 1:4.

5. Paul sent him on special assignments to Corinth to straighten things out when they were having problems and experiencing unruliness in the fellowship.

    - See:

        2 Corinthians 7:13-14.

        2 Corinthians 8:6.

        2 Corinthians 8:16.

6. Paul actually considered Titus to be a faithful, intelligent partner who understood the faith and God's Word who correctly and effectively communicated it just as well as Paul did.

- See:
- 2 Corinthians 8:23.
- 2 Corinthians 12:18.

7. The way Paul spoke of Titus as a partner or fellow fiduciary of God's Word went far beyond that of a fellow worker or companion.

8. When Paul arrived in Troas he had no peace of mind about the situation in Corinth so he left and went to find Titus in Macedonia before continuing with his work.

   - See 2 Corinthians 2:12-13.

9. Titus achieved a great deal in Corinth as Paul had hoped.

   - See 2 Corinthians 7:5-16.

10. Paul traveled to Crete with Titus and left him there to complete the same type of difficult work he had handled in Corinth.

    - See Titus 1:5.

11. The entire letter to Titus shows him in charge of yet another difficult situation. Here we see Paul instructing him to put an end to the trouble there. Paul referred to the inexcusable problems that Titus needed to deal with on Crete in no uncertain terms. He applied God's standard as found in His Word and communicated it as such instead of trying to be palatable or "politically correct" to the offenders. He was not concerned about being overly sensitive to those who were being incalcitrant. Instead, he was concerned about setting things aright for the good and faithful on Crete and correcting or weeding out those following unbiblical principles and causing problems.

- See the whole of the letter to Titus.

At this point you may well be asking what was so important and difficult about Crete?

Crete is Greece's largest island. It encompasses 3,219 square miles of varied terrain including fine-sand beaches as well as the White Mountains. After the Trojan war the principal cities formed themselves into a number of independent republics. These republics included Knossos, Cydonia and Gortyna. (Local fellowships of believers seem to have developed in all of these locales.) The ancient Roman Empire had annexed the entire island of Crete around 67 B.C. Its modern-day capital is the city of Herklion which today boasts of the Heraklion Archaelogical Museum housing many ancient Minoan artifacts.

Crete is also the source of many myths and legends from the ancient past. It is the traditional birthplace of the supreme Greek god, Zeus. (Interestingly, the website https://www.incrediblecrete.gr/cretan-mythology/ makes the astounding claim that "Cretans are the genuine descendants of the Cretan-born Zeus, the god of gods, humans and hospitality." Apparently the culture today is not all that different than that confronted by Paul and Titus.

The legends and myths surrounding this island are often encountered in various textbooks on mythology as well as TV cartoon series such as Clash of the Titans and Hercules, and include:

1. The ingenious craftsman Daedalus who is credited with building the famous Labyrinth.

2. Multiple ancient goddesses including those related to animals, fertility, snakes and the supposed mother of Zeus.

3. King Minos of Knossos who appeared in Homer's Illiad and Odyssey and according to legend conquered the Aegean pirates and established a navy.

4. The Minotaur, a monstrous animal with the head of a bull and the body of a man, which was imprisoned in the Labyrinth.

5. Icarus, who supposedly attempted to fly away with wax wings which melted when he got too close to the sun, plunging him into what became known as the Icarian Sea.

6. Ancient "robots" in ancient legend repeated as such by Plato and Socrates.

With this backdrop of the strange, macabre, and what some would even say verges on the demonic, no wonder Crete was such a hard place to work.

It is also of note that the ancient Philistines and Philistia as mentioned numerable places in Scripture had their genesis as a colony of Crete. This is not the time or place for an in-depth study of the subject. However, one might profit from a review of the historical information contained in the most historically accurate book in existence, which we call the Bible. I might suggest that one begin with Jeremiah 47 and put all the attendant verses of the Tanakh together to gain a more full understanding of the history, culture and society on Crete.

CALL A SPADE A SPADE
TITUS 1:1-16

Preface: The title to this session may seem strange to some without the benefit of history as it relates to the English language. The term, "call a spade a spade" or more fully on an historical basis "let's call a spade a spade, not a gardening tool" came into common usage in the English language in 1542 and actually emanates from the classical Greek of Plutarch's *ApophthegmataLaconica*. The idiom has appeared in many classical works including those of the famous authors Ralph Waldo Emerson, Jonathan Swift, W. Somerset Maugham, Oscar Wilde, and Charles Dickens.

The intent behind the idiom and the import is that one should call something by a name that communicates its true and correct description and not employ some flowery description that actually obfuscates the truth.

I am reminded of a time many years ago when a friend was visiting the home where I grew up. The friend was a huge, as in size and relative skill, athlete and was also somewhat socially inept when it came to the opposite sex. He had started to date an attractive woman he met who he said worked at the local Harley shop. I knew of this woman, a consort of a local biker gang, who was allegedly involved in a number of less than civil and tasteful activities. (I am, by this description, not "calling a spade a spade.")

When my friend mentioned he was dating her in the presence of my mother, who surprisingly also knew about the activities of this woman, and asked if we were familiar with her, my mother said something along the lines of "I hear she has had a very interesting life." At that point in my life, wanting to protect my friend from what could have been a very bad experience, I became irritated with my mother for what I felt was hiding the truth. I said, "That's not what you heard about her" and proceeded to give a full description of what I knew to be this woman's proclivities and activities from personal observation. My mother was not pleased with me, but in the end my friend was grateful and went on to eventually find and marry a beautiful and committed believer. My mother, in this instance, did not "call a spade a spade," but I most assuredly did.

By the way, we should also mention, that in 1928 a writer used the term "spade" as an ethnic slur against African Americans. This has absolutely nothing to do with the saying, but the existence of this term in the colloquial speech of some people has led to the original idiom being used less often than it was previously.

Paul, in his letter to Titus, was most definitely "calling a spade a spade" in the most direct and proper terms to help his partner understand and appropriately address the situation with which he was faced. This is in concert with the whole of God's Word where we find truth on a high pedestal and lies or liars condemned to hell.

Read the following verses to see what else we learn in God's Word about lies, liars, and our speech.

Proverbs 13:5

Proverbs 12:22

Colossians 3:9

Exodus 23:1

1 Timothy 1:8-10

Revelation 21:8

Proverbs 6:16-19

1 Corinthians 6:9-11

James 1:26

1 Peter 3:10

Proverbs 30:5-6

Ephesians 4:15-16

Proverbs 12:19

Colossians 4:5-6

Ephesians 4:29-30

How does God regard liars?

Why do you think God speaks of liars as being on a par with murderers and those who are sexually immoral?

Conversely, what does God expect from the speech of a believer?

Open in Prayer

Group Warm-Up Questions

What characteristics do you think are necessary in a good leader?

What leader has had the most influence on you? How?

Read: Titus 1:1-16

Reread: Titus 1:1

How does Paul describe himself in the opening line of this letter?

Also read:

Titus 1:1 (Again)

John 14:6

John 17:17

How does he describe the task he has been given?

Please make a list.

1.

2.

3.

Reread: Titus 1:2

What is one of the primary functions of the truth in the life of a believer?

When was this promised to those who trust God though His Son?

What is one thing God cannot and will not do?

Reread: Titus 1:3

At what time did God reveal His special message?

By whose command was Paul entrusted with the announcement of His message?

To whom is this message to be announced?

Reread: Titus 1:4

To whom was Paul writing?

What was Paul's relationship to Titus?

What did they share?

What, in particular, did Paul wish for Titus?

Why do you think he wished him these specific things in light of the situation in which Titus found himself?

Reread: Titus 1:5

Why did Paul leave Titus in Crete?

Reread: Titus 1:5 and Titus 1:10

Note: It was Paul's practice to appoint elders or leaders in the churches he helped start. He had not been able to stay long enough in Crete to evaluate the situation and the potential "applicants" to get this done.

Why, in particular, was it necessary at this time to appoint elders in the various towns on Crete?

Why is it necessary to appoint leaders in any group of human beings?

Why is it particularly important to have good leaders in groups of believers?

What happens to any group of people that does not have good leaders?

Reread: Titus 1:6-9

Also read: 1 Timothy 3:2-3

God had provided us with two categories of characteristics that should or should not be present in the lives of those serving as church leaders or elders. To better understand this, please construct the two following lists from the text.

Characteristics that should be Evident in a Leader or Elder

1.

2.

3.

4.

5.

6.

7.

8.

9.

10.

11.

12.

13.

14.

Characteristics that should NOT be Evident in a Leader or Elder

1.

2.

3.

4.

5.

6.

7.

Reread: Titus 1:6

Why do you feel it is necessary that a leader in the body of believers act or not act in these ways?

Reread: Titus 1:7

Why do you think it is necessary that a leader among believers exhibit or not exhibit these characteristics?

Note 1: Reading this verse in the King James translation of the bible reveals the genesis of the term "filthy lucre," which we sometimes encounter in literature. Please take a look at this and discuss what you take it to mean.

Note 2: The Greek words used in the original language of the material under consideration today for leaders and elders are *episkopos* (bishop-Titus 1:7 KJV and NKJV) and *presbuteros* (elder-Titus 1:7 Aramaic Bible in Plain English). These designations for overseers incorporate the ideas of a person who is mature both physically and spiritually.

Note 3: This verse also puts a leader among believers in the position of a "fiduciary." This concept has application in the financial, legal and other aspects of society. It is a concept on which I have lectured to Certified Public Accountants, attorneys, and financial professionals while providing continuing education in many states over the years.

It was codified in an 1830 court ruling, but as we can see in God's Word the concept has existed throughout human history.

In the financial world it was originally called the "prudent man rule."

As times changed and people became more aware, its approbation morphed into the "prudent person rule."

In current usage it has developed further into the "prudent expert rule" and indicates that one should use the care and diligence of a prudent expert when acting in the interest of another party.

A fiduciary's responsibilities or duties are both ethical and legal. When a party knowingly accepts a <u>fiduciary position</u> on behalf of another party, they are required to act in the best interest of the principal.

Strict care must be taken to ensure no <u>conflict of interest</u> arises between the fiduciary and the principal.

Take a look at the following references to see this concept illustrated in God's Word. Please make note of what you see in each case.

Genesis 39:1-9

1 Corinthians 4:1-2

Luke 16:1-13

Matthew 25:21

John 3:27

Reread: Titus 1:8

Why are these characteristics so important in the life of a leader in the body of believers?

Reread: Titus 1:9

Why is it a requirement that a leader in the body of believers exhibit these specific characteristics?

Why can a person not be a good and competent leader if these characteristics are lacking in their life?

With what work in the body of believers has God entrusted you?

How can you encourage other believers with different roles than you?

Reread: Titus 1:10

Note: Paul said there were some "rebellious" (Titus 1:10 NIV, NLT, NASB, BSB) people in the fellowship on Crete. These people were self-appointed leaders and attempting to usurp authority within the fellowship for themselves. Some say this is too kind a definition to use in describing what they were doing. Again, I am not completely "calling a spade a spade."

What were three of the things these problematic people were doing?

1.

2.

3.

How should such rebellious people in the fellowship of believers be treated today?

We should also note that God deals with this subject extensively in his Word.

While the following verses are not exhaustive, they do provide a foundation of knowledge, information and instruction about how to regard and handle such people and problems when they inevitably arise. If these verses sound familiar you might realize we referenced many of them in our study of the fourth chapter of Paul's first letter to Timothy.

Matthew 7:15-16

Ephesians 5:11

Galatians 1:8

Matthew 16:12

Leviticus 18:29 (For context and application see Leviticus 18:1-30.)

Romans 16:17-18

1 Kings 22:46

Titus 3:10-11

2 Thessalonians 3:6

1 Corinthians 15:33

Hebrews 6:4-6

1 Corinthians 5:1-6

Numbers 15:30

1 Corinthians 5:9-13

Titus 2:7-8

2 Timothy 4:2-4

Ephesians 4:14-15

2 Timothy 2:15

Acts 17:11

Reread: Titus 1:11

What was the result of what these negative people were doing as it related to some families in the fellowship?

How were these families being influenced?

Why were the problematic pretenders doing and saying the things they were?

What did Paul tell Titus that he must do with these trouble makers?

Reread: Titus 1:12

Note: Paul is here quoting Epimenides, a poet born on Crete centuries earlier.

How did this man describe his countrymen?

Note 2: At the time Paul wrote this letter to Titus a word in common usage in Greek was *kretizein*. It literally means to "speak like a Cretan," which was synonymous with being a liar.

Note 3: We might also notice that Paul was not content to refer to these people as "liars" (Titus 1:12 GNB), "gluttons" (Titus 1:12 GNB), and "animals" (Titus 1:12 NLT). He went one step further and referred to them as "cruel or evil animals" (Titus 1:12 NLT) and "lazy gluttons" (Titus 1:12 ESV, NLT, BSB, NIV, GNB). (You may want to look at this verse in several translations to get the full measure of Paul's feeling.)

Why do you think he felt so strongly about these people?

Reread: Titus 1:13

How did Paul feel about the general populace of Crete?

What did he again tell Titus to do in regard to the actual believers who were being misled?

What did Paul hope would be the result of reprimanding these people?

Read:

Jude 1:3

Acts 18:24-26

How do you see these verses tying into what we see in Titus 1:13?

What do you perceive to be the responsibility of every believer in this regard?

Reread: Titus 1:14

What else did Paul say those being misled by false teachers must do?

Do you think the history of Crete with its strange myths had anything to do with believers there being so vulnerable and misled?

Reread: Titus 1:15

What do we learn in this verse about:

1. Those whose hearts are pure?

2. Those who are corrupt and unbelieving? (Please fill in the blanks below.)

    1. _____ is pure to them.

    2. Their _____ have been corrupted.

    3. Their _____ have been corrupted.

What does it mean to you that "everything is pure to those who are pure" (Titus 1:15 NLT)? How does this evidence itself in everyday life?

What does it mean to you that "nothing is pure to those who are corrupt and unbelieving" (Titus 1:15 NLT)? How do you see this in the lives of such people?

Note: Just so we have no doubt, God has given us even more guidance and information specifically about deceivers who have been used by our enemy while masquerading in fellowships of believers. While we find this in many places in God's Word, He here summarizes it quite succinctly.

Note 2: We should also realize that this verse is quite often misapplied and used by some people to justify ungodly practices that are in direct conflict with the whole of God's Word. Paul, in this verse, was referring to the false teaching of legalists as it related to dietary laws. The verse cannot be used to justify pornography or adultery, although there are some barely scripturally literate individuals who try to do so.

Read the following verses for a greater understanding of this and discuss:

What they meant to the people at the time they were written.

What they mean to us today.

2 Timothy 4:3-4

Matthew 15:8-20

1 Timothy 6:3-5

Galatians 6:7

Galatians 1:6-9

2 Peter 2:1

Matthew 5:18

Isaiah 5:20

Isaiah 40:8

Acts 17:11

James 1:22

Psalm 119:160

2 Peter 3:16-17

Deuteronomy 4:2

Deuteronomy 12:32

Proverbs 30:5-6

Revelation 22:18-19

Reread: Titus 1:16

What are the five hallmarks Paul herein mentions of the type of deceptive, destructive people causing trouble among the believers on Crete?

1.

2.

3.

4.

5.

Note: The fellowship of believers on Crete was obviously somewhat new and not yet sufficiently grounded in God's Word. Read the following verses to see what would eventually happen to them as they studied the Scriptures, engaged in prayer and continued to fellowship with other people who had trusted in Yeshua Ha-Maschiach, the Jewish Messiah.

Romans 12:2

Ephesians 6:10-18

2 Timothy 3:16-17

Please list the results of this ongoing process as you see it from these references:

1.

2.

3.

4.

5.

6.

7.

8.

9.

10.

11.

12.

13.

14.

15.

What do your actions reveal about your relationship with God?

Application Questions

What area of your character most needs your attention at this point in your life?

What is one way you can support biblical principles, true doctrine, and sound teaching in the fellowship or church of which you are a part?

How can you show support for leaders in your fellowship who are following biblical standards of teaching and action?

What can you do to encourage another believer in his or her faith this week?

Close in Prayer

TEACH THEM WELL
TITUS 2:1-15

Open in Prayer

Group Warm-Up Questions

How do parents teach their children their values and beliefs?

What religious beliefs were you taught growing up? How?

If the things you were taught when growing up later seemed to be untrue, how did it impact you?

Read: Titus 2:1-15

Reread: Titus 2:1

What kind of living did Paul direct Titus to promote?

How do you see this working?

Does this seem to you to be backwards? Does right teaching promote right living or do they somehow go together? Please explain.

What does a person's lifestyle reveal about his or her beliefs?

Read: Proverbs 16:21

How do you see this relating to the concept we are now discussing?

Why is it so important in helping people incorporate definitive biblical principles in their lives?

Please explain how you see this working.

What examples can you think of when this occurred in a helpful fashion?

When have you seen this not happening in a fashion that was not only not helpful, but destructive?

Reread: Titus 2:2

How should older men conduct themselves?

1.

2.

3.

4.

5.

6.

Reread: Titus 2:3

How should older women live?

1.

2.

3.

4.

Reread: Titus 2:4-5

What additional responsibility do these older women have? Please make a list.

1.

2.

3.

4.

5.

6.

7.

Note: You might recall from other studies in this series that the biblical concept of submission is a military term and means to do things in order with an effective command structure.

What is the consequence if older women do not do these above eleven things?

How does it bring shame on the Word of God if older women do not act as prescribed in the Judeo-Christian Scriptures?

Does this also apply to the actions of younger women, older men, and younger men? How so?

Reread: Titus 2:6

What are young men encouraged to do?

How do the admonitions in the previous verses apply to younger men?

Reread: Titus 2:2-5

Also read:

Colossians 3:23-24

Colossians 4:5-6

Ephesians 4:29-30

Philippians 4:8

1 Samuel 15:22

In your own words, how would you describe the kind of lifestyle a follower of Jesus Christ should exhibit?

Reread: Titus 2:7-8

What did Paul tell Titus to do?

1.

2.

3.

4.

Please take the above principles which you have extracted from God's Word and discuss how each one works.

How does this relate to leaders today?

What happens when leaders live in this fashion?

What happens when leaders do not live this way?

What happens when one's teaching is "so correct that it cannot be criticized?"

How do you think the Scriptures might define teaching that is correct in this fashion?

Read the following verses as you construct your answer.

Proverbs 16:21

Acts 17:11

Do you think all believers, whether they are in the role of teachers or not, have this same responsibility to God as well as to each other? Please explain.

How do you see these concepts operating to enable believers to help each other remain accountable and faithful?

Reread: Titus 2:9-10

Note: Paul, at this point, gives Titus instructions for slaves. We should realize that in today's parlance this might also include employees.

What did he tell slaves or perhaps employees today, they must not do?

1.

2.

Conversely, what did he tell them that they absolutely had to do?

1.

2.

What is the result when slaves or employees act as God herein instructs in His Word?

What can you do to make the truth of God and His Word attractive to those who do not know Him by the way you live? Please explain.

Reread: Titus 2:11

What does the grace of God bring?

To whom is this gift brought?

Reread: Titus 2:12-13

From what are believers to turn?

1.

2.

On the other hand, what characteristics should be evident in the way believers live?

1.

2.

3.

4.

Reread: Titus 2:14

Inherent in this verse is the statement that Jesus gave His life for each and every one of us while we did not deserve it. This act, if acknowledged and responded to with trust in Him, has several general and life-enhancing results. What are they as listed here?

1.

2.

3.

4.

What motivates you personally to live a godly life?

How do you define such a life?

Reread: Titus 2:15

What did Paul tell Titus he must do?

1.

2.

3.

4.

What did Paul remind Titus about the authority that he (Titus) had?

Do leaders in the faith have this same responsibility and authority today?

Why is it so important that leaders do these things in the face of so much strange and false teaching in the world today?

What is to be the ultimate source of what leaders in the faith are to teach?

Read 2 Timothy 3:16-17 as you construct your answer.

Why must this be the crucible of all teaching, truth and action for those following God?

Read Acts 17:11 yet again as you think about your answer.

What specific things that you have learned in your life about being faithful to God and His Word can you share with younger believers to encourage them?

Application Questions

Is there a specific adjustment in your life or comportment that might make you a more effective communicator of the life available by God and revealed through His Word?

How can you remind yourself each day that the way you work is a positive or negative testimony to others?

What step can you take in your life to share what you have learned as a believer with a person to whom it might be helpful who is on the same journey, albeit at an earlier time in their experience?

Close in Prayer

WEEK 16
ACT LIKE A REAL BELIEVER
TITUS 3:1-15

Open in Prayer

Group Warm-Up Questions

What is the dirtiest job you ever had to do?

In your opinion, how can an argument damage a friendship?

Read: Titus 3:1-15

Note: The title of today's study comes not only from Paul and Timothy, but from other believers, including Larry Norman, the "Father of Christian Rock." Larry was fed up with people who gave lip service to Jesus but then lived their lives as if they never heard of Him. In one of his recordings he said "Be a real Christian baby," which was followed by his description of someone not living a life consistent with the Judeo-Christian Scriptures. And with that we will take a look at the last portion of Paul's letter to Titus where this sentiment was echoed in relationship to the trouble makers Titus had to deal with on Crete.

Reread: Titus 3:1

How does God want us to submit to authority?

Why is this sometimes difficult?

What are we to do if those in authority are requiring believers to act in opposition to the principles of life and action so clearly laid out in the Word of God?

Read Acts 5:27-29 as you put together your answer.

Consider how Polycarp, a leader among the early followers of the Jewish Messiah, dealt with an extreme situation of this nature.

The Smyrnans readily accepted Caesar worship. In 196 B.C. they erected a temple to Dea Roma, the goddess of Rome and subsequently built one to Tiberius. Worship of the Roman emperor was compulsory. Each year a Roman citizen had to burn a pinch of incense on the altar to acknowledge publicly that Caesar was the supreme lord. In return, the citizen received a formal certificate that he had done so. Originally this action was intended to simply prove one's political loyalty and unify the empire since citizens were free to worship whatever gods they desired so long as they acknowledged the emperor as number one. However, this test became a vital one for followers of Jesus Christ, many of whom refused to perform this ritual and were consequently burned at the stake or savagely torn apart by wild beasts in the arena.

About 160 years after the birth of Christ, the bishop of Smyrna, a man named Polycarp, refused to acknowledge the emperor as his lord. When he was offered the chance to recant his faith and deny Jesus Christ he said, "Eighty and six years have I served Him, and he never did me wrong. How can I now speak evil of my King who has saved me?" The old man was burned at the stake on the Sabbath day.

Polycarp's death and suffering as well as that of many other believers who perished in similar circumstances could have been avoided had they simply put a pinch of incense on the altar acknowledging the Roman emperor as lord. Instead, they remained faithful to the King of the Universe.

There were, however, some so-called Christians, who did put a pinch of incense on the altar and received a certificate saying they did in fact recognize Caesar as lord. They rationalized this action by saying to themselves or perhaps even to God that they didn't really mean it. One can only imagine how the true Lord of all felt about this cowardly action on the part of these weak-kneed people. Actually, we don't need to wonder what Jesus thought about this. We can clearly see what he said when he walked the face of the earth in the following references.

Matthew 10:32–33

32 "Everyone who acknowledges me publicly here on earth, I will also acknowledge before my Father in heaven. 33 But everyone who denies me here on earth, I will also deny before my Father in heaven." NLT

Matthew 10:28

"Don't be afraid of those who want to kill your body; they cannot touch your soul. Fear only God, who can destroy both soul and body in hell." NLT

What should be the overriding marks of the conduct of a believer?

Read: Philippians 3:20

How are believers not absolved from responsibility toward authorities on earth even though our citizenship resides in heaven? Please explain.

Note: Several years ago I had a friend by the name of Aaron Zelman. He was involved in an excellent civil rights organization that he founded that went by the initials JPFO. I was one of the charter members and was asked to do an interview for *USA Today* regarding their work. After over fifteen years of success Aaron decided that he and the organization should go one step further and advise their members to stop paying taxes since he felt the governing authorities were no longer serving the interests of the people. Sadly, after discussing this in depth with Aaron, I found it necessary to withdraw my support for any such endeavor by the organization. It ultimately led to their decline and Aaron's premature passing.

Do you think Aaron was right or wrong? Why?

Do you think I was right or wrong? Why?

Reread: Titus 3:2

What things should not be part of the normal discourse for a follower of the Jewish Messiah?

Conversely, what characteristics should be evident in the conduct, speech and lives of believers?

This verse actually says a believer should show true humility to everyone, regardless of their station in life. How does this work in real life when someone is trying to quarrel with us?

In this verse we see slander and quarreling spoken of as the opposites of gentleness and humility. Why do you think this is so? Please explain.

Note: It is an interesting quirk of human nature that people often accord rumors and things told them in secret as truth without verification. We can see this in the old saying, "Some people will believe anything if it is whispered to them." Why do you think this is often the case?

How can we guard against this?

Read: 2 Timothy 1:7

How can a believer show gentleness, humility and power all at the same time in their relationships with other people?

Reread: Titus 3:3

What does this verse say we were like before making an overt decision to trust in Jesus?

It is possible that some readers may feel they were guilty of none of the things noted as having existed in the lives of unbelievers in this verse. If that is so for you, do you think you exhibited some of the traits mentioned in any way? For your convenience I have listed them below. In each case please consider them and note how each was or is applicable to you. (Note: This list is private and not intended to be shared unless you feel comfortable doing so.)

Foolish

Applicable or not?

How so?

Disobedient

Applicable or not?

How so?

Misled

Applicable or not?

How so?

Slaves of Many Lusts

Applicable or not?

How so?

Slaves of Many Pleasures

Applicable or not?

How so?

Life Full of Evil

Applicable or not?

How so?

Life Full of Envy

Applicable or not?

How so?

Life Full of Hate

Applicable or not?

How so?

Hated One Another

Applicable or not?

How so?

Reread: Titus 3:3-7

If you have become a believer, what happened when you trusted Jesus Christ, the Jewish Messiah, on a personal basis? (Please put this succinctly in your own words in a version that might be pleasantly shared in an interesting fashion with someone who has not yet had this privilege.)

Reread: Titus 3:4

What happened to those who have had the above mentioned experience?

What saved Paul from his "foolishness?"

How is it even possible that Paul had foolishness from which to be saved knowing that he was perhaps the most intelligent and highly educated person of his time?

Read the following verses as you think about this:

Philippians 3:4-8

Acts 22:3

1 Corinthians 1:25

Reread: Titus 3:5

When it says "He saved us," (Titus 3:5 NASB) what does it mean? Please explain in your own words.

What did we do to deserve this?

Why did God do this for us?

This verse also lays out 3 very important and specific components of this experience. Please list them.

1.

2.

3.

Read:

Galatians 5:22-23

1 Corinthians 2:10

John 14:26

John 16:13

How would you describe the role of the Holy Spirit in this process?

Why is it important that God saves us not because we deserve it, but because of His great mercy?

How should this impact our lives?

Reread: Titus 3:6

What does God generously pour out upon us when we trust in Jesus Christ?

Reread: Titus 3:7

What quality of God made it possible for Him to do so many good things for us?

Note: In this passage we see both God's grace and mercy mentioned. These two related concepts can be succinctly defined as follows:

Grace is defined as getting what you don't deserve.

Mercy is defined as not getting what you do.

How do you see these two concepts operating in your life?

Reread: Titus 3:7

Specifically what did God do for those who have trusted in Him through Jesus? Please enumerate:

1.

2.

3.

Reread: Titus 3:8

In your own words, considering what we have studied so far in this chapter, what are the trustworthy teachings Titus is to insist upon?

In addition to these teachings, how does Paul tell Titus he should act?

Should we teach and act the same as Titus? Please explain how and why.

Read: James 2:14-20

What else does James tell us about the importance of doing good?

What does it show if we do not live our lives according to the Words of Life found in Scripture?

Conversely, how does a life well-lived both confirm and give real meaning to one's faith in practical terms?

Reread: Titus 3:9

What kind of discussions, quarrels and fights are counter-productive for a believer to be involved with?

Why are such things a waste of time?

Note: We should also realize that in saying this Paul knew that he personally could win any such arguments. He just knew doing so would not be helpful to him or any other participants (see Philippians 3:4-6).

Warren Wiersbe felt that such debates never helped anyone come any closer to God. In fact, he went so far as to claim that people claiming to be believers who liked to argue in the fashion mentioned in Titus 3:9 were, in his opinon:

1. Usually covering up some sinful practice in their lives.

2. Insecure.

3. Unhappy at work.

4. Unhappy at home.

What are your thoughts about his experience with such people? Do you feel he was generally right or wrong?

Can you think of an example that bears out your opinion? Please elaborate.

Reread: Titus 3:10

How did Paul say Titus should deal with people causing divisions in the way he described?

Should we do the same?

Difficulties with people of this nature are not new. They have plagued those who would follow God from time immemorial. As you might expect, Scripture is replete with information about how to effectively deal with this situation. See the following verses for some further instructional guidelines:

Proverbs 13:20

Proverbs 14:7

Proverbs 25:26

Psalm 1:1-4

Psalm 119:115

Psalm 26:4-5

1 Corinthians 5:11-13

1 Corinthians 5:13

2 Corinthians 6:14

2 Peter 3:17

Numbers 16:1-35

How do you see this working out in actual practice?

What happens if we ignore the biblical admonition about how to conduct things within the structure of a group of believers? Please give an example.

Reread: Titus 3:11

What else do we learn about people who cause divisions the way some people were in Crete?

Why was it especially important that Titus take this to heart as he cleaned up the troubled fellowship on Crete?

Reread: Titus 3:12

Which of his special fellow workers was Paul considering sending to help Titus?

Note: Artemas is thought to have been not only one of the 72 disciples sent out personally by Jesus Christ in Luke 10:1-20, but was also known to have served as the Bishop of the fellowship of believers in Lystra.

We read about Tychicus in many places such as Colossians 4:7. He was a trusted messenger, leader and trouble shooter on "Paul's team."

Knowing this, why might Paul have particularly wanted to send one of these two men?

Where did Paul want to stay for the winter?

Note: Nicopolis was destroyed by a great earthquake in 499 A.D., so most people today have never heard of it except for obscure historical references such as the one we find here.

In its day, however, it was a nice place and would have been a pleasant spot for Paul to spend the winter.

It was founded in 29 BC by Caesar Augustus in commemoration of his victory in 31 BC over Antony and Cleopatra at the Battle of Actium nearby. It became a major city of the region and sported a 77 row theatre, an aqueduct, hot baths, and stadium. At the time of its prominence it constituted a major transportation and communications link between the eastern and western halves of the Mediterranean.

Many impressive ruins of the city can still be seen today.

Reread: Titus 3:13

Who did Paul want Titus to be sure and help?

Note: Apollos was an Alexandrian Jew with an extensive knowledge of the Old Testament. This depth of knowledge made him extremely popular with the many other Jewish believers to the point that he put off a trip to Corinth so as not to interfere with what Paul was doing. We see him mentioned in:

Acts 18:24-26

1 Corinthians 3:4-6

1 Corinthians 16:12

Zenas, a contraction for Zenodorus, was a Jewish scribe and an expert in the Hebrew law.

From the way in which these two followers of the Jewish Messiah are mentioned in this verse it appears that they may have actually personally delivered the letter from Paul to Titus.

Reread: Titus 3:14

What did Paul say believers must do?

Besides performing a vital function, what did such activity prevent?

Does this principal still work in today's world? How so?

Reread: Titus 3:15

Who sent their greetings to the believers on Crete?

To whom were these greetings sent?

Why do you think these greetings were sent to this specific group of people and not to the general population of Crete?

How did Paul conclude his letter?

Please redefine grace from earlier in this session.

What do you feel was the significance of this conclusion?

Application Questions

What steps can you take in your interactions with others to be sure your conversations are meaningful, interesting, and effective?

What can you do this week to reconcile a damaged relationship?

How can you say thank you to God this week for His saving grace toward you?

Close in Prayer

APPENDIX 1

HOW TO AVOID ERROR

(Partially excerpted from *The Road to Holocaust* by Hal Lindsey)

1. The most important single principle in determining the true meaning of any doctrine of our faith is that we start with the clear statements of the Scriptures that specifically apply to it, and use those to interpret the parables, allegories and obscure passages. This allows Scripture to interpret Scripture. The Dominionists (and others seeking to bend Scripture to suit their purposes) frequently reverse this order, seeking to interpret the clear passages using obscure passages, parables and allegories.

2. The second most important principle is to consistently interpret by the literal, grammatical, historical method. This means the following:

   1. Each word should be interpreted in light of its normal, ordinary usage that was accepted in the times in which it was written.

287

2. Each sentence should be interpreted according to the rules of grammar and syntax normally accepted when the document was written.

3. Each passage should also be interpreted in light of its historical and cultural environment.

Most false doctrines and heresy of Church history can be traced to a failure to adhere to these principles. Church history is filled with examples of disasters and wrecked lives wrought by men failing to base their doctrine, faith, and practice upon these two principles.

The Reformation, more than anything else, was caused by an embracing of the literal, grammatical, and historical method of interpretation, and a discarding of the allegorical method. The allegorical system had veiled the Church's understanding of many vital truths for nearly a thousand years.

Note 1: It is important to note that this is how Jesus interpreted Scripture. He interpreted literally, grammatically, and recognized double reference in prophecy.

Note 2: It is likewise important that we view Scripture as a whole. Everything we read in God's Word is part of a cohesive, consistent, integrated message system. Every part of Scripture fits in perfectly with the whole of Scripture if we read, understand, and study it properly.

Note 3: Remember to **<u>Appropriate the power of The Holy Spirit.</u>**

Read: Luke 11:11-13

Read: I Timothy 4:15-16

Read: Luke 24:49

Read: II Peter 2:1

Read: John 7:38-39

Read: Mark 13:22

Read: John 14:14-17, 26

APPENDIX 2

UNDERSTANDING COMPOSITE PROBABILITY AND APPLYING IT TO THE JUDEO-CHRISTIAN SCRIPTURES

Before proceeding we might briefly reflect upon the reliability of the Judeo-Christian Scriptures. All honest researchers into their veracity have found that, as historical documents, they are without parallel. They are the most reliable and incontrovertibly accurate documents available in the world today. This has been the conclusion of all the erudite scholars and investigators who have taken the time to delve into this topic. For more information on this subject you may wish to read *The Case For Christ* by Lee Stroebel, *More Than a Carpenter* by Josh McDowell, and the *Evidence That Demands a Verdict* series, also by Josh McDowell. This is, of course, a very short list of the volumes available. A great deal of augmentative and corroborative material is available in such volume that if one were so inclined they might spend a lifetime in its study.

To better understand one of the ways the Creator of the Universe has validated His Word and the work and person of Jesus Christ, it is helpful to get a grasp on composite probability theory and its application to the Judeo-Christian Scriptures.

We are indebted to Peter W. Stoner, past chairman of the Department of Mathematics and Astronomy at Pasadena City College as well as to Dr. Robert C. Newman with his Ph.D. in astrophysics from Cornell University for the initial statistical work on this topic. Their joint efforts on composite probability theory were first published in the book *Science Speaks*.

Composite Probability Theory

If something has a 1 in 10 chance of occurring, that is easy for us to understand. It means that 10 percent of the time, the event will happen. However, when we calculate the probability of several different events occurring at the same time, the odds of that happening increase exponentially. This is the basic premise behind composite probability theory.

If two events have a 1 in 10 chance of happening, the chance that both of these events will occur is 1 in 10 x 10, or 1 in 100. To show this numerically this probability would be 1 in 10^2, with the superscript indicating how many tens are being multiplied. If we have 10^3, it means that we have a number of 1000. Thus 10^4 is equivalent to 10,000 and so on. This is referred to as 10 to the first power, 10 to the second power, 10 to the third power, and so on.

For example, let's assume that there are ten people in a room. If one of the ten is left handed and one of the ten has red hair, the probability that any one person in the room will be left handed and have red hair is one in one hundred.

We can apply this model to the prophecy revealed in the Bible to figure out the mathematical chances of Jesus' birth, life and death, in addition to many other events occurring in the New Testament by chance. To demonstrate this, we will consider eight prophecies about Jesus and assign a probability of them occurring individually by chance. To eliminate any disagreement, we will be much more limiting than is necessary. Furthermore, we will use the prophecies that are arguably the most unlikely to be fulfilled by chance. I think you will agree that in doing so, we are severely handicapping ourselves.

1. The first prophecy from Micah 5:2 says, "But you, O Bethlehem Ephrathah, are only a small village in Judah. Yet a ruler of Israel will come from you, one whose origins are from the distant past" (NLT). This prophecy tells us that the Messiah will be born in Bethlehem. What is the chance of that actually occurring? As we consider this, we also have to ask: What is the probability that anyone in the history of the world might be born in this obscure town? When we take into account all of the people who ever lived, this might conservatively be 1 in 200,000.

Amazingly, about 700 years after this prophecy was uttered it was fulfilled when Yeshua Ha-Maschiach (The Jewish Messiah), who we call Jesus, was born in exactly the place predicted. We see this in Luke 2:11 where it states "The Savior—yes, the Messiah, the Lord—has been born today in Bethlehem, the city of David" (NLT)!

2. Let's move on to the second prophecy in Zechariah 9:9: "Rejoice greatly, O people of Zion! Shout in triumph, O people of Jerusalem! Look, your King is coming to you. He is righteous and victorious, yet He is humble, riding on a donkey---even on a donkey's colt" (NLT). For our purposes, we can assume the chance that the Messiah (the King) riding into Jerusalem on a donkey might be 1 in 100. But, really, how many kings in the history of the world have actually done this?

The fulfillment of this particular prophecy 500 years later was so unnerving that Matthew, Mark, Luke and John all included it in their historical accounts.

Matthew recorded it as "Tell the people of Jerusalem, 'Look, your King is coming to you. He is humble, riding on a donkey—riding on a donkey's colt'" (Matthew 21:5 NLT).

This appears in John's writings as "The next day, the news that Jesus was on the way to Jerusalem swept through the city. A large crowd of Passover visitors took palm branches and went down the road to meet him. They shouted, "Praise God! Blessings on the one who comes in the name of the LORD! Hail to the King of Israel!" Jesus found a young donkey and rode on it, fulfilling the prophecy that said: "Don't be afraid, people of Jerusalem. Look, your King is coming, riding on a donkey's colt" (John 12:12–15 NLT).

3. The third prophecy is from Zechariah 11:12: "I said to them, 'If you like, give me my wages, whatever I am worth; but only if you want to.' So they counted out for my wages thirty pieces of silver" (NLT). What is the chance that someone would be betrayed and the price of that betrayal would be thirty pieces of silver? For our purposes, let's assume the chance that anyone in the history of the world would be betrayed for thirty pieces of silver might be 1 in 1,000.

As unlikely as it may have seemed on the surface, this prediction was fulfilled approximately 500 years later and was noted by Matthew with the language itself being eerily similar to what had been written so many years ago. The NLT shows this as "How much will you pay me to betray Jesus to you? And they gave him thirty pieces of silver." (Matthew 26:15) How shocking would it be if you found that someone predicted exactly what you were going to spend for your next dinner out 500 years ago?

4. The fourth prophecy comes from Zechariah 11:13: "And the Lord said to me, 'Throw it to the potter'---this magnificent sum at which they valued me! So I took the thirty coins and threw them to the potter in the Temple of the Lord" (NLT). Now we need to consider what the chances would be that a temple and a potter would be involved in someone's betrayal. For our statistical model, let's assume this is 1 in 100,000.

This prophecy and its fulfillment is a continuation and completion of the one immediately prior to it in which the exact amount of the bribe for the betrayal of the Jewish King was predicted, again 500 years before it occurred. Here we find predicted not only the betrayal and the exact payment, but the actual usage of the funds. Matthew records fulfillment of this whole process as "I have sinned," he declared, "for I have betrayed an innocent man." "What do we care?" they retorted. "That's your problem." Then Judas threw the silver coins down in the Temple and went out and hanged himself. The leading priests picked up the coins. "It wouldn't be right to put this money in the Temple treasury," they said, "since it was payment for murder." After some discussion they finally decided to buy the potter's field, and they made it into a cemetery for foreigners (Matthew 27:4-7 NLT).

5. The fifth prophecy in Zechariah 13:6 reads: "And one shall say unto him, What are these wounds in thine hands? Then he shall answer, Those with which I was wounded in the house of my friends" (KJV). The question here is, "How many people in the history of the world have died with wounds in their hands?" I believe we can safely assume the chance of any person dying with wounds in his or her hands is somewhat greater than 1 in 1,000.

Again, 500 years later we see this specific prophecy fulfilled and the evidence viewed by Jesus's disciples in John 20:20 where it says "As he spoke, he showed them the wounds in his hands and his side. They were filled with joy when they saw the Lord" (NLT)!

6. The sixth prophecy in Isaiah 53:7 states, "He was oppressed and treated harshly, yet he never said a word. He was led like a lamb to the slaughter. And as a sheep is silent before the shearers, he did not open his mouth" (NLT). This raises a particularly tough question. How many people in the history of the world can we imagine being put on trial, knowing they were innocent, without making one statement in their defense? For our statistical model, let's say this is 1 in 1,000, although it is pretty hard to imagine.

In this case, approximately 700 years passed between the time the prediction was made and we see it fulfilled in Mark 15:3-5. There it is recorded as "Then the leading priests kept accusing him of many crimes, and Pilate asked him, "Aren't you going to answer them? What about all these charges they are bringing against you?" But Jesus said nothing, much to Pilate's surprise" (NLT).

7. Moving on to the seventh prophecy, Isaiah 53:9 says "He had done no wrong and had never deceived anyone. But he was buried like a criminal; he was put in a rich man's grave" (NLT). Here we need to consider how many people, out of all the good individuals in the world who have died, have died a criminal's death and been buried in a rich person's grave. These people died out of place. (Some might also infer that they were buried out of place, though that is not necessarily true.) Let's assume the chance of a good person dying as a criminal and being buried with the rich is about 1 in 1,000.

Again we find that 700 years passed between the prediction of this event and the actual occurrence. Again, this event was so momentous that it was recorded by Matthew, Mark, Luke and John. Astonishingly, we find that he was placed in the tomb by not just one person of wealth, but by two. Joseph of Arimathea and Nicodemus, two of the wealthiest men in the region, worked together and laid the body in Joseph's own tomb. Matthew 27:60, speaking of Joseph of Arimathea's part in entombing Jesus' body says, "He placed it in his own new tomb, which had been carved out of the rock. Then he rolled a great stone across the entrance and left" (NLT).

8. The eighth and final prophecy is from Psalm 22:16: "My enemies surround me like a pack of dogs; an evil gang closes in on me. They have pierced my hands and feet" (NLT). Remember this passage and all the other prophetic references to the crucifixion were written before this form of execution was invented. However, for our purposes, we just need to consider the probability of someone in the history of the world being executed by crucifixion. Certainly, Jesus wasn't the only person killed by being crucified. We will say that the chances of a person dying from this specific form of execution to be at 1 in 10,000.

Here we might note that Psalm 22 was penned by King David approximately 1000 years prior to the birth of Jesus. The word "crucifixion" and its derivatives had not yet been coined, but we see the process described in detail. Again, because of the import of this event it is recorded by each of the Gospel writers. In Mark 16:6 we see the fulfillment of the ancient prophecy and more where we read, "Don't be alarmed. You are looking for Jesus of Nazareth, who was crucified. He isn't here! He is risen from the dead! Look, this is where they laid his body" (NLT).

Calculating the Results

To determine the chance that all these things would happen to the same person by chance, we simply need to multiply the fraction of each of the eight probabilities. When we do, we get a chance of 1 in 10^{28}. In other words, the probability is 1 in 10,000,000,000,000,000,000,000,000,000.

Would you bet against these odds?

Unfortunately, there is another blow coming for those who do not believe the Bible is true or Jesus is who He said He was. There are not just eight prophecies of this nature in the Bible that were fulfilled in Jesus Christ------there are *more than three hundred* such prophecies in the Old Testament. The prophecies we looked at were just the ones that we could *most easily* show fulfilled.

If we deal with only forty-eight prophecies about Jesus, based on the above numbers, the chance that Jesus is not who He said He was or the Bible is not true is 1 in 10^{168}. This is a larger number than most of us can grasp (though you may want to try to write it sometime). To give you some perspective on just how big this number is, consider these statistics from the book *Science Speaks* by Peter Stoner:

- If the state of Texas were buried in silver dollars two feet deep, it would be covered by 10^{17} silver dollars.

- In the history of the world, only 10^{11} people have supposedly ever lived. (I don't know who counted this.)

- There are 10^{17} seconds in 1 billion years.

- Scientists tell us that there are 10^{66} atoms in the universe and 10^{80} particles in the universe.

- Looking at just forty-eight prophecies out of more than three hundred, there is only a 1 in 10^{168} chance of Jesus not being who He said He was or of the Bible being wrong.

In probability theory, the threshold for an occurrence being absurd---translate that as "impossible"---is only 10^{50}. No thinking person who understands these probabilities can deny the reality of our faith or the Bible based on intellect. Every person who has set out to disprove the Judeo-Christian Scriptures on an empirical basis has ended up proving the Bible's authenticity and has, in most cases, become a believer.

These facts are more certain than any others in the world. However, not everyone who has come to realize the reliability and reality of these documents has become a believer. These intelligent people who understand the statistical impossibility that Jesus was not who He claimed to be and who yet do not make a decision for Christ are not senseless; they generally just have other issues. They allow these issues to stop them from enjoying the many experiential benefits that God offers them through His Word and the dynamic relationship they could have with Him, not to mention longer-term benefits. These people, of course, deserve love and prayer, because this is not just a matter of the intellect. If it were, every intelligent inquirer would be a believer. Rather, it is very much a matter of the heart, the emotions, and the spirit.

The truth of this statement was brought home to me in one very poignant situation. In this case, someone very near and dear to me said, "But Dad, this could have been anybody." No, this could not have been just anybody. The chance these prophecies could have been fulfilled in one person is so remote as to be absurd. That is impossible. Only one person in human history fulfilled these prophecies and that person is Jesus Christ. To claim otherwise is not intelligent, it is not smart, it is not well-considered, and it is not honest. It may be emotionally satisfying, but in all other respects it is self-delusional.

Lightning Source UK Ltd.
Milton Keynes UK
UKHW030630080121
376670UK00010B/1173